A Fly in the Soup

POETS ON POETRY

David Lehman, General Editor
Donald Hall, Founding Editor

New titles

Tess Gallagher, *Soul Barnacles*
Rachel Hadas, *Merrill, Cavafy, Poems, and Dreams*
Larry Levis, *The Gazer Within*
Ron Padgett, *The Straight Line*
Charles Simic, *A Fly in the Soup*

Recently published

Edward Hirsch, *Responsive Reading*
John Koethe, *Poetry at One Remove*
Yusef Komunyakaa, *Blue Notes*
Philip Larkin, *Required Writing*
Alicia Suskin Ostriker, *Dancing at the Devil's Party*
James Tate, *The Route as Briefed*

Also available are collections by

A. R. Ammons, Robert Bly, Philip Booth, Marianne Boruch,
Hayden Carruth, Fred Chappell, Amy Clampitt, Tom Clark,
Douglas Crase, Robert Creeley, Donald Davie, Peter Davison,
Tess Gallagher, Suzanne Gardinier, Allen Grossman, Thom Gunn,
John Haines, Donald Hall, Joy Harjo, Robert Hayden,
Daniel Hoffman, Jonathan Holden, John Hollander,
Andrew Hudgins, Josephine Jacobsen, Weldon Kees,
Galway Kinnell, Mary Kinzie, Kenneth Koch, Richard Kostelanetz,
Maxine Kumin, Martin Lammon (editor), David Lehman,
Philip Levine, John Logan, William Logan, William Matthews,
William Meredith, Jane Miller, Carol Muske, John Frederick Nims,
Geoffrey O'Brien, Gregory Orr, Marge Piercy, Anne Sexton,
Charles Simic, Louis Simpson, William Stafford, Anne Stevenson,
May Swenson, Richard Tillinghast, Diane Wakoski, C. K. Williams,
Alan Williamson, Charles Wright, and James Wright

Charles Simic

A Fly in the Soup

MEMOIRS

Ann Arbor

THE UNIVERSITY OF MICHIGAN PRESS

2003   2002   2001   2000   4   3   2   1

A CIP catalog record for this book is available
from the British Library.

Library of Congress Cataloging-in-Publication Data

Simic, Charles, 1938–
    A fly in the soup : memoirs / Charles Simic.
        p.   cm.
    — (Poets on poetry)
    ISBN 0-472-11150-7 (alk. paper)
    1. Simic, Charles, 1938–   2. Poets, American—20th
century—Biography.   I. Title.   II. Series.
PS3569.I4725 Z468   2000
811'.54—dc21   00-09295

Acknowledgments

Portions of *A Fly in the Soup* were previously published in Charles Simic's *Wonderful Words, Silent Truth: Essays on Poetry and a Memoir* (University of Michigan Press, 1990); *The Unemployed Fortune-Teller: Essays and Memoirs* (University of Michigan Press, 1994); and *Orphan Factory: Essays and Memoirs* (University of Michigan Press, 1997). Other portions appeared originally in different form as "With Gene Tierney in Paris" in *O.K., You Mugs: Writers on Movie Actors,* edited by Luc Sante and Melissa Holbrook Pearson (Pantheon, 1999); and as "Refugees" in *Letters of Transit,* edited by Andre Acimen (The New Press, 1999).

"Letter to Simic from Boulder" is from *Making Certain It Goes On: The Collected Poems of Richard Hugo.* Copyright © 1984 by the Estate of Richard Hugo. Reprinted by permission of W. W. Norton and Company, Inc.

1

Don't tell me the plot . . . I'm just a bit-player.

—Raymond Chandler

Mine is an old, familiar story by now. So many people have been displaced in this century, their numbers so large, their collective and individual destinies so varied, it's impossible for me or any one else, if we are honest, to claim any special status as a victim. Particularly, since what happened to me fifty years ago is happening to someone else today. Rwanda, Bosnia, Afghanistan, Kosovo, the endlessly humiliated Kurds—and so it goes. Fifty years ago it was fascism and communism, now it's nationalism and religious fundamentalism that make life miserable in lots of places. Recently, for instance, I was translating the work of a woman poet from Sarajevo for an anthology and its editors had great difficulties locating her. She had vanished. She was not a young woman, she had plenty of friends, but no one seemed to know what had happened to her in the confusion of the war.

"Displaced persons" (DP) is the name they had for us back in 1945, and that's what we truly were. As you sit watching bombs falling in some old documentary or the armies advancing against each other, villages and towns going up in fire and smoke, you forget about the people huddled in the cellar. Mr. and Mrs. Innocent and their families paid dearly in this century for just being there. Condemned by history, as Marxists were fond of saying, perhaps belonging to a wrong class, wrong ethnic group, wrong religion—and what have you—they were and continue to be an unpleasant reminder of all the philosophical and nationalist utopias gone wrong. With their rags and bundles and their general air of misery and despair, they came in droves from the East, fleeing evil with no idea where they were running to. No one had much to eat in Europe, and here were the starving refugees, hundreds of thousands of them in trains, camps, and prisons, dipping stale bread into watery soup, searching for lice on their children's heads, and squawking in dozens of languages about their awful fate.

My family, like so many others, got to see the world for free, thanks to Hitler's wars and Stalin's takeover of East Europe. We were not German collaborators or members of the aristocracy, nor were we strictly speaking political exiles. Small fry, we made no decisions ourselves. It was all arranged for us by the world leaders of the times. Like so many others who were displaced, we had no ambition to stray far beyond our neighborhood in Belgrade. We liked it fine. Deals were made about spheres of influences, borders were redrawn, the so-called Iron Curtain was lowered, and we were set adrift with our few possessions. Historians are still documenting all the treacheries and horrors that came our way as the result of Yalta and other such conferences, and the subject is far from finished.

As always, there were degrees of evil and degrees of tragedy. My family didn't fare as badly as others. The Allies returned to Stalin against their will hundreds of thousands of Russians whom the Germans had forcibly brought to work in their factories and on their farms. Some were shot and the rest packed off to the gulags so they would not contaminate the rest of the citizenry with newly acquired decadent capitalist notions. Our own prospects were rosier. We had hopes of ending up in the United States, Canada, or Australia. Not that this was guaranteed. Getting into the United States was especially difficult. Most Eastern European countries had very small quotas, unlike the Western European ones. Southern Slavs, in the eyes of the American genetic experts and immigration policy makers, were not a highly desirable ethnic material.

It's hard for people who have never had the experience to truly grasp what it means to lack proper documents. We read every day about our own immigration officers using and misusing the recently acquired authority to turn back suspicious aliens from our borders. The pleasure of humiliating the powerless must not be underestimated. Even as a young boy, I could see that was the case. Wherever there are bureaucrats, the police state is an ideal.

I remember standing in endless lines in Paris at the police headquarters to receive or renew resident permits. It seems like that's all we ever did when we lived there. We'd wait all day only to discover that the rules have changed since the last time, that they now require, for instance, something as absurd as my mother's parents' marriage certificate or her grade school diploma, even though she is in possession of a French diploma, since she did her postgraduate studies in Paris. As we'd stand there pondering the impossibility of what they are asking of us, we'd be listening to someone at the next window trying to convey in poor French how their house burned, how they left in a hurry with only one small suitcase, and so on, to which the official would shrug his shoulders and proceed to inform them that, unless the documents are produced promptly, the residence permit will be denied.

So, what did we do? Well, if the weather was nice, we'd go and sit on a street bench and watch the lucky Parisians stroll by carrying groceries, pushing baby carriages, walking their dogs, even whistling. Occasionally, a couple would stop in front of us to smooch, while we cursed the French and our rotten luck. In the end we'd trudge back to our small hotel room and write home.

The mail doesn't travel very swiftly, of course. We go nuts every day for weeks waiting for the mailman, who can't stand the sight of us since we are always pestering him, and still, somehow, the documents arrive, thanks to a distant relative. Then they had to be translated by an official translator, who, of course, couldn't make heads or tails out of the dog-eared fifty-year-old entry in a provincial Balkan school or church registry. In any case, eventually we'd go back to the long line only to discover that they were not needed after all, but something else was. Every passport office, every police station, every consulate, had a desk with a wary and bad-tempered official who suspected us of not being what we claimed to be. No one likes the refugee. The ambiguous status of being called a DP made it even worse. The officials we met knew next to nothing about where we came from and why, but that did not prevent them from passing judgment on us. Being driven out by the Nazis brought out a measure of sympathy, but leaving because of the

Communists was not as well received. If the officials were left-ists, they told us bluntly that we, ungrateful wretches that we were, had left behind the most progressive, the most just, society on the face of the earth. The others figured we were just riffraff with fake diplomas and a shady past. Even the smiling dummies in store windows on the elegant Avenue Victor Hugo regarded us as if we were out to steal something. It was actually all extremely simple: either we were going to get a foothold here or somewhere else, or we were going back to a refugee camp, prison, or, even worse, to "the embodiment of man's dearest longing for justice and happiness," as the Communist world was described in certain quarters.

Immigration, exile, being uprooted and made a pariah, may be yet the most effective way devised to impress on an individual the arbitrary nature of his or her own existence. Who needs a shrink or a guru when everyone we met asked us who we were the moment we opened our mouths and they heard the accent.

The truth is, we had no simple answers. Being rattled around in freight trains, open trucks, and ratty ocean liners, we ended up being a puzzle even to ourselves. At first, that was hard to take; then we got used to the idea. We began to savor it, to enjoy it. Being nobody struck me personally as being far more interesting than being somebody. The streets were full of these "somebodys" putting on confident airs. Half of the time I envied them; half of the time I looked down on them with pity. I knew something they didn't, something hard to come by unless history gives you a good kick in the ass: how superfluous and insignificant in any grand scheme mere individuals are! How pitiless are those who have no understanding that this could be their fate too.

2

I have a photograph of my father wearing a black tuxedo and holding a suckling pig under his arm. He's on stage. Two dark-eyed beauties in low-cut party dresses are standing next to him and giggling. He's laughing too. The pig has its mouth open, but it doesn't look as if it's laughing.

It's New Year's Eve. The year is 1928. They are in some kind of nightclub. At midnight the lights were turned off, and the pig was let loose. In the pandemonium that ensued, my father caught the squealing animal. It was now his. After the bows, he got a rope from the waiter and tied the pig to the leg of their table.

He and the girls visited several other establishments that night. The pig went with them on a rope. They made it drink champagne and wear a party hat. "Poor pig," my father said years later.

At daybreak they were alone, the pig and my father, drinking in a low dive by the railroad station. At the next table a drunken priest was marrying a young couple. He crossed the knife and fork to bless the newlyweds. My father gave them the pig as a wedding present. Poor pig.

That's not the end of the story, however. In 1948, when my father was already on his way to America and we were starving back in Belgrade, we used to barter our possessions for food. You could get a chicken for a good pair of men's shoes. Our clocks, silverware, crystal vases, and fancy china were exchanged for bacon, lard, sausages, and such things. Once an old Gypsy wanted my father's top hat. It didn't even fit him. With that hat way down over his eyes, he handed over a live duck.

A few weeks later his brother came to see us. He looked prosperous. Gold teeth in front, two wristwatches, one on each hand. The other, it seems, had noticed a tuxedo we had. It was true. We let these people walk from room to room appraising the merchandise. They made themselves at home, opening drawers, peeking into closets. They knew we wouldn't object. We were very hungry.

Anyway, my mother brought out the 1926 tuxedo. We could see immediately the man was in love with it. He offered us first one, then two chickens for it. For some reason my mother got stubborn. The holidays were coming. She wanted a suckling pig. The Gypsy got angry, or pretended to be. A pig was too much. My mother, however, wouldn't give in. When she set her mind to it, she could really haggle. Years later in Dover, New Hampshire, I watched her drive a furniture salesman nuts. He offered to give her the couch for free just to get rid of her.

The Gypsy was tougher. He marched out. Then, a few days later, he came back to take another look. He stood looking at the tux my mother had in the meantime brushed off. He looked, and we looked. Finally, he let out a big sigh like a man making a difficult and irreversible decision. We got the pig the next day. It was alive and looked just like the one in the picture.

3

In the beginning . . . the radio. It sits on the table by my bed. It has a dial that lights up. The stations' names become visible then. I can't read yet, but I make others read them to me. There's Oslo, Lisbon, Moscow, Berlin, Budapest, Monte Carlo, and still many more. One aligns the red arrow with a name, and a strange language and unfamiliar music burst forth. At ten o'clock the stations sign off. The war is on. The year is 1943.

The nights of my childhood were spent in the company of that radio. I attribute my lifelong insomnia to its temptations. I couldn't keep my hands off it. Even after the stations went silent, I kept turning the dial and studying the various noises. Once I heard beeps in Morse code. Spies, I thought. At times I'd catch a distant station so faint I'd have to press my ear against the rough burlap that covered the speaker. Somewhere dance music was playing, or the language was so appealing I'd listen to it for a long time, feeling myself on the verge of understanding.

All this was strictly forbidden. I was supposed to be asleep. Come to think of it, I must have been afraid to be alone in that big room. The war was on. The country was occupied. Terrible things happened at night. There was a curfew. Someone was late. Someone else was pacing up and down in the next room. Black paper curtains hung over the windows. It was dangerous even to peek between them at the street—the dark and empty street.

I see myself on tiptoes, one hand on the curtain, wanting to look but afraid of the light the radio tubes cast dimly through its trellised back onto the bedroom wall. My father is late, and outside the roofs are covered with snow.

On April 6, 1941, when I was three years old, the building across the street was hit by a bomb at five in the morning and set on fire. Belgrade, where I was born, has the dubious distinction of having been bombed by the Nazis in 1941, by the Allies in 1944, and by NATO in 1999. The number of dead for that day in April in what was called by the Germans "Operation Punishment" ranges between five thousand and seventeen thousand, the largest number of civilian deaths in a single day in the first twenty months of war. The city was attacked by four hundred bombers and over two hundred fighter planes on a Palm Sunday when visitors from the countryside swelled the capital's population. Whatever the true count is, Luftwaffe Marshal Alexander Lohr was tried for terror bombing and hung in 1945.

Sometimes I think I remember nothing about that bomb, and sometimes I see myself on the floor with broken glass all around me, the room brightly lit and my mother rushing to me with outstretched arms. I was later told that I was thrown out of my bed and across the room when it landed and that my mother, who was sleeping in the next room, found me thus. Whenever I asked her to elaborate, she refused, giving me one of her habitual sighs and looks of exasperation. It's not so much that the memory was traumatic for her—it certainly was! What upset her and made her speechless on the subject was the awful stupidity of it all. My father believed in fighting for a just cause. She, on the other hand, never swayed from her conviction that violence and especially violence on this scale was stupid. Her own father had been a colonel in World War I, but she had no illusions. War was conducted by stern men with rows of medals on their chests who never really grew up. If you mentioned an Allied victory to her, she'd remind you of how many mothers on both sides had lost their sons.

I have another vague memory of bright flames and then enveloping darkness as I was being rushed down the stairs of our building into the cellar. That happened many times during World War II, so it may have been on another occasion. What surprised me years later, when I saw a German documentary footage of the bombing, was to find a brief shot of my street with several additional buildings destroyed in the neighborhood. I didn't realize until that very moment how many bombs had rained on my head that morning.

Many people died in the building across the street, including one family who had a boy my age. For some reason the subject kept coming up years later. I was told again and again what a nice family they were and what a beautiful boy he was and how he even looked a little bit like me. I found it very spooky, but the story was retold with an air of obliviousness as to what this may mean to me. I have no idea what he may have looked like, as I have no idea what I looked like at a young age, but I kept seeing him as I grew even more clearly as if he had been my playmate once.

Was the world really so gray then? In my early memories it's almost always late fall. The soldiers are gray, and so are the people.

The Germans are standing on the corner. We are walking by. "Don't look at them," my mother whispers. I look anyway, and one of them smiles. For some reason that makes me afraid.

One night the Gestapo came to arrest my father. They were rummaging everywhere and making a lot of noise. My father was already dressed. He was saying something, probably cracking a joke. That was his style. No matter how bleak the situation, he'd find something funny to say. Years later, surrounded by doctors and nurses after having suffered a serious heart attack, he replied to their "How're you feeling, sir?" with a request for pizza and beer. The doctors thought he had suffered brain damage. I had to explain that this was normal behavior for him.

I guess I went back to sleep after they took him away. In any case, nothing much happened this time. He was released. It wasn't his fault his kid brother stole a German army truck to take his girlfriend for a spin. The Germans were astonished, almost amused, by the audacity. They shipped him off to work in Germany. They made the attempt, that is, but he slipped through their fingers.

Our wartime equivalent of jungle gyms, slides, tree houses, forts, and mazes were to be found in that ruin across the street. There was a part of the staircase left. We would climb up between the debris, and all of a sudden there would be the sky! One small boy fell on his head and was never the same again. Our mothers forbade us to go near that ruin; they threatened us, tried to explain the many perils awaiting us, and still we went. Sitting blissfully in what was left of someone's third-floor dining room, we would hear one of our mothers shrieking on the street below and pointing in our direction while her son scurried down struggling to remember where he put his foot on the way up.

We played soldiers. The war went on, bombs fell, and we played soldiers. We machine-gunned each other all day long. Rat-tat-tat! We dropped dead on the sidewalk. We ran through the crowd imitating the sound of fighter planes diving and strafing.

Then we became bomber planes. We dropped things from a window or a balcony on people in the street. A bomb's friend is gravity, I remember reading once in some army manual. Bombs are either carried under the wing or in a special compartment inside the plane. As for us, we only had to spread our arms, rev up the motors, and windmill around while holding an object in our hands until it was time to release our payload. One of my friends even had military goggles, which he let us borrow occasionally. It made bombing the street below even more authentic in our eyes.

That *boom-boom* sound comes naturally to the male species. It's a rare girl that can make the noise properly. We threw gravel on people passing below, bricks on stray cats and dogs, pretending we were dropping American bombs on the Nazis. Fifty years later I still remember the illicit pleasure and the malice of doing that. Now that video games are available on which one can enact the NATO bombing of Yugoslavia, children discuss knowingly bombs guided by lasers and TV cameras. I think we had a clearer idea of what hitting a building really means, and still that didn't stop us. We were as heedless as today's generals pressing a button and watching the computer screen excitedly for the outcome.

The British and the Americans started bombing Belgrade on Easter Sunday, April 16, 1944. The official version from the United States Air Force speaks about heavy bombers "conducting strikes against Luftwaffe and aviation targets" with "approximately 397 tons of bombs." It also says: "According to one report, these operations of 17 of April resulted in some damage to a residential area northwest of BELGRADE/ZEMUN AIRDROME. Most of the destruction wrought by the two days' activities, however, appears to have been military in nature." It's that word *appears,* judiciously inserted in the report, that is the crux of the matter.

It was just before lunchtime. The dining room table was already set in a festive way with our best china and silverware when the planes came. We could hear them drone even before the sirens wailed. The windows were wide open, since it was a balmy spring day. "The Americans are throwing Easter eggs," I remember my father shouting from the balcony. Then we heard the first explosions. We ran down to the same cellar, where today some of the original cast of characters are still cowering. The building shook. People covered their ears. One could hear glass breaking somewhere above. A boy a little older than I had disappeared. It turned out that he had slipped out to watch the bombs fall. When the men brought him back, his mother started slapping him hard and yelling she's going to kill him if he ever does that again. I was more frightened of her slaps than of the sound of the bombs.

At some point it was all over. We shuffled out. The enthusiasts of aerial bombardment either lack imagination for what happens on the ground, or they conceal their imaginings. The street was dark with a few flames here and there. With all the dust and smoke in the air, it was as if the night had already fallen. A man came out of the gloom covered with fallen plaster, telling us that a certain neighborhood had been entirely leveled. This was typical. One heard the most outrageous rumors and exaggerations at such times. Thousands of deaths, corpses lying everywhere, and so forth. It was one of the poorest parts of the city he was talking about. There were no military objects there. It didn't make any sense even to a child.

The day after the first raid in 1944, the planes came again, and it was more of the same. "They dropped about 373 tons of bombs on the BELGRADE/SAVA MARSHALLING YARDS," the official report continues. "This assault resulted in major destruction of freight and passenger cars, large fires, gutted warehouses, severe damage to the main passenger station, equally severe damage to the railroad bridge over the Sava River, etc. No report on this mission refers to the bombing of other than military objectives." Actually, a bomb landed on our sidewalk in front of our building. It spun around but didn't explode.

Some nights my father refused to go down to the cellar. He stayed in bed, while my mother screamed from the stairs for him to come down. She was for fleeing the city immediately; my father thought being in the countryside was equally dangerous with a civil war in progress. So, with our allies' bizarre targeting, it was hazardous to stay and equally hazardous to go. That whole spring and summer of 1944 we trekked back and forth, mostly on foot. I remember columns of refugees on the roads, the Germans checking documents and frightening everybody even more. Today, of course, there's television to record such unhappy sights.

In 1972 I met one of the men who bombed me in 1944. I had just made my first trip back to Belgrade after almost twenty years. Upon my return to the States, I went to a literary gathering in San Francisco, where I ran into the poet Richard Hugo in a restaurant. We chatted, he asked me how I spent my summer, and I told him that I had just returned from Belgrade.

"Oh yes," he said, "I can see that city well."

Without knowing my background, he proceeded to draw on the tablecloth, among the breadcrumbs and wine stains, the location of the main post office, the bridges over the Danube and Sava, and a few other important landmarks. Without a clue as to what all this meant, supposing that he had visited the city as a tourist at one time, I inquired how much time he had spent in Belgrade.

"I was never there," he replied. "I only bombed it a few times."

When absolutely astonished, I blurted out that I was there at the time and that it was me he was bombing, Hugo became very upset. In fact, he was deeply shaken. After he stopped apologizing and calmed down a little, I hurried to assure him that I bore no grudges and asked him how is it that they never hit the

Gestapo headquarters or any other building where the Germans were holed up. Hugo explained that they made their bombing runs from Italy, going first after the Romanian oil fields, which had tremendous strategic importance for the Nazis and were heavily defended. They lost a plane or two on every raid, and with all that, on the way back, they were supposed to unload the rest of the bombs over Belgrade. Well, they didn't take any chances. They flew high and dropped the remaining payloads any way they could, anticipating already being back in Italy, spending the rest of the day on the beach in the company of some local girls.

I assured Hugo that this is exactly what I would have done myself, but he continued to plead for forgiveness and explain himself. He grew up in a tough neighborhood in Seattle, came from poor, working-class folk. His mother, a teenager, had to abandon him after his birth. We were two befuddled bit players in events beyond our control. He at least took responsibility for his acts, which of course is unheard of in today's risk-free war, where the fashion is to blame one's mistakes on technology. Hugo was a man of integrity, one of the finest poets of his generation, and, strange as it may appear, it did not occur to me to blame him for what he had done. I would have probably spat in the face of the dimwit whose decision it was to go along with Tito's request and have the Allies bomb a city on Easter full of its own allies. Still, when Hugo later wrote a poem about what he did and dedicated it to me, I was surprised. How complicated it all was, how inadequate our joint attempt to make some sense of it in the face of the unspoken suspicion that none of it made a hell of a lot of sense.

Letter to Simic from Boulder

Dear Charles: And so we meet once in San Francisco and I
    learn
I bombed you long ago in Belgrade when you were five.
I remember. We were after a bridge on the Danube
hoping to cut the German armies off as they fled north
from Greece. We missed. Not unusual, considering I
was one of the bombardiers. I couldn't hit my ass if
I sat on the Norden or rode a bomb down singing

The Star Spangled Banner. I remember Belgrade opened
like a rose when we came in. Not much flak. I didn't know
about the daily hangings, the 80,000 Slav who dangled
from German ropes in the city, lessons to the rest.
I was interested mainly in staying alive, that moment
the plane jumped free from the weight of bombs and we went
    home.
What did you speak then? Serb, I suppose. And what did your
    mind
do with the terrible howl of bombs? What is Serb for "fear"?
It must be the same as in English, one long primitive wail
of dying children, one child fixed forever in dead stare.
I don't apologize for the war, or what I was. I was
willingly confused by the times. I think I even believed
in heroics (for others, not for me). I believed the necessity
of that suffering world, hoping it would learn not to do
it again. But I was young. The world never learns. History
has a way of making the past palatable, the dead
a dream. Dear Charles, I'm glad you avoided the bombs, that
    you
live with us now and write poems. I must tell you though,
I felt funny that day in San Francisco. I kept saying
to myself, he was on the ground that day, the sky
eerie mustard and our engines roaring everything
out of the way. And the world comes clean in moments
like that for survivors. The world comes clean as clouds
in summer, the pure puffed white, soft birds careening
in and out, our lives with a chance to drift on slow
over the world, our bomb bays empty, the target forgotten,
the enemy ignored. Nice to meet you finally after
all the mindless hate. Next time, if you want to be sure
you survive, sit on the bridge I'm trying to hit and wave.
I'm coming in on course but nervous and my cross hairs flutter.
Wherever you are on earth, you are safe. I'm aiming but
my bombs are candy and I've lost the lead plane. Your friend,
    Dick.

My grandfather had a summerhouse not far from Belgrade.
When we arrived there after two days of bombs, my father's side
of the family had already assembled. They argued all the time.

In addition to the German occupation, a civil war was going on in Yugoslavia. There were at least a half-dozen factions made up of Royalists, Communists, Fascists, and various other collaborators, all slaughtering each other. Our family was bitterly divided between the Royalists and the Communists. My grandfather remained neutral. They were all the same in his opinion.

As for my mother, she said nothing. She disliked my father's people. She came from an old middle-class family, while they were blue-collar workers. She was educated in Paris, while they sat around getting drunk in taverns. That's how she saw it. It's astonishing that she and my father ever got together. My father had gone to the university and was now a successful engineer, but he had an equally low opinion of my mother's world.

It wasn't long before he left us. Early one morning my mother and I accompanied him to the small and crowded train station. By the way he looked at us, and by the way he hugged me, I knew this was no ordinary journey. I was told nothing. Ten years would pass before I would see him again. People would ask, "Where's your father?" and I couldn't tell them. All my mother knew that day was that he was attempting to go to Italy, but there was no news of him for a long time.

We stayed with my grandparents. Summer came. The bombing of Belgrade continued occasionally. We could see the planes high over the city. Our house was on a hill overlooking the River Sava and had a fine view in that direction. Columns of smoke went up as the bombs fell. We'd be eating watermelon in our garden, making pigs of ourselves while watching the city burn. My grandmother and mother couldn't bear it and would go inside with the dog, who also did not like it. My grandfather insisted that I sit by his side. He'd cut me a little cheese, give me a sip of red wine, and we would strain to hear the muffled sound of explosions. He didn't say anything, but he had a smile on his face that I still remember. My father's father had a dark view of the human species. As far as he was concerned, we were all inmates in a nuthouse. Events like this confirmed what he already suspected. In the meantime, there were the night scents of a country garden in full bloom, the stars in the sky, the silence of a small village. No birds peeping, no cats fighting or dogs barking. Just my grandmother, every now and then, opening the front door to a creak and pleading with us to please come indoors.

The garden was overgrown with tall sunflowers and weeds. I'd go hide among them, even though there were rattlesnakes, especially in the rockpile under my window. I'd sit on the steps talking to them while they hissed back. Once I threw a stone at one, missed, and worried it would come that night and visit me in my bed.

I slept and went around naked. It was so hot. The river was close by, but we only went to dip our feet. There were corpses in it. Every few days they would fish one out. Some people didn't care. One evening I saw some young women splashing under the willows in their slips, but, when I drew close to take a better look, I saw a couple of armed men sitting in the shadows and smoking. Their beaus, I presumed.

That one time I was alone for some reason. Mostly, I was not allowed to wander around. The world was full of bad people. A man attacked a boy my age who lived across the street by biting him on his neck. It happened in broad daylight as he stood in front of his house.

For days on end I did nothing but stay in my room playing. I remember lying on the floor eye to eye with one of my toy soldiers or watching flies walk across the ceiling. Except for these few scattered images, I have no idea what I thought, what I felt.

One night a munitions factory several miles away was blown up. Again I was thrown out of bed. The room was lit up. Night had turned into day. We sat up till dawn watching the fiery sky. In the morning there was a big movement of troops. They went around confiscating the few domestic animals that were still around. Afterward, you could not hear a hen cackle, a rooster crow, anywhere.

The fighting was intensifying. The Russian army was in southern Romania pushing toward Belgrade along the Danube. Locally, the various political and guerilla factions were settling scores. There was a lot of indiscriminate killing. After I found some bodies in the roadside ditch near our house, I was not allowed to go out anymore. Our neighbors were executed in their own home. The people across the street just disappeared. Nothing happened to us. My mother was very pregnant and wobbled around. She had no politics, and neither did my grandfather. That doesn't explain it, of course. We were just lucky, I guess.

It was a relief when the Russians finally came. At least now there were only two sides fighting. The Germans had retreated across the river from us. One could see them go about their business, bringing up some artillery pieces. The Russians had their own guns just above our house. It was clear, if both sides started shooting, we'd be right in the middle.

Pregnant as she was, my mother decided to flee to a village further up beyond the hill where we knew some people. My grandparents retreated to the cellar.

It was mid-October 1944. The road to the village was empty, and so was the farmhouse of our friend, where we found only a very old woman, who gave us some goat's milk. That whole day we sat in the kitchen with that silent old woman and waited for the people to come back. I remember the chill, the gray light in the window, and how my mother kept reminding me to keep quiet.

Toward dusk we heard steps. A wild-looking man with blood on his face told us, without even stopping, that the Germans were coming this way and killing everybody in sight. There was nothing else to do but hurry back to my grandfather's house. The old woman stayed behind. We were back on the empty road lined with poplars. It was so quiet we could hear our quick steps. All of a sudden there were shots. A bullet whizzed by. My mother pulled me to the ground and threw herself over me. Then it was quiet again. Just our hearts beating. No more shots.

After a long time, we raised our heads. It had cleared up. The sky was cloudless. The first few evening stars were in their places. We rose slowly and stood in the deep shadow of the trees. Then we resumed our way under the cover of darkness. When we got back, my grandfather was sitting at the table, drinking a toast with a Russian officer, and grinning at us.

My wartime adventures really began the day the Russians liberated Belgrade. We had gotten back to our apartment through the rubble of fighting and celebrating crowds, since my mother wanted to be near her doctor. The very next day she managed somehow to get herself a cot in the basement of a private clinic in order to await the termination of her pregnancy. As it turned out, she stayed there a month. I was entrusted to the care of one of my mother's aunts, the only relative we had left in the city.

Nana was the black sheep in the family. It was whispered that she cheated on her old husband, was spending his money recklessly, and used bad language. That's what I loved about her. This elegant, good-looking woman would swear often and shamelessly.

I've no idea where Nana's husband was or why she was still in the city. I suspect she had her own private reasons. This was the second day of the liberation, and there were still Germans holed up in the neighborhood, fighting. To my surprise she allowed me to go out on the street alone. There were other children out there, to be sure, but, still, this was strange. Often I'd return home and find no one. Later, I would see her returning home, beautifully dressed, wearing gloves and high heels on the sidewalk strewn with broken glass and plaster. She'd be glad to see me and would have something special for me to eat, some unheard-of delicacy like chocolate filled with nuts or smoked sausage.

Strangely enough, she never went out at night. I've no memory of what we did in the evenings. Our building was almost empty. The lights were mostly out. There was nothing to do but sleep a lot. One morning, on awakening early, I saw my aunt washing her breasts in a pail of cold water. She caught me watching her and turned around. She burst out laughing and did a little dance, naked like that.

I was happy. My friends and I had plenty to do during the day and plenty of time to do it in. There was no school, and our parents were either absent or busy. We roamed the neighborhood, climbed over the ruins, and watched the Russians and our partisans at work. There were still German snipers in a couple of places. We'd hear shots and take off running. There was a lot of military equipment lying around. The guns were gone, but there was other stuff. I got myself a German helmet. I wore empty ammo belts. I had a bayonet.

One day I was sitting with a friend in front of our building when a column of German prisoners came by, escorted by some women soldiers. "Hey kids, let's go and shoot some Germans!" said one cheerily. Well, this is a bit too much. We said nothing. Actually, I doubt that I gave them a straight answer. One learned early to be circumspect and cautious. Never volunteer information, keep your mouth shut—that sort of thing. We followed them as far as the corner and then turned back. I remember one tall, blond German, straight as a broomstick. The others looked humpbacked in comparison.

Later, we went there anyway. There was an old cemetery nearby with a huge church and beyond it the fairgrounds, where supposedly all the shootings took place. We met a pack of children on the way who said that they were from the circus. It was true. There used to be a circus tent on the fairgrounds in the early years of the war, but now only a few trailers were left on its edge. These were odd-looking children. They wore the strangest clothes—unmatched, wrong-sized costumes—and they jabbered, speaking a foreign language among themselves.

"Show him what you can do," said my friend, who had met them before. They obliged. A little boy stood on his hands. Then he removed one hand and was left for a moment standing on the other. A thin, dark-eyed, dark-haired girl leaned back until her head emerged from between her legs.

"They have no bones," my friend whispered. The dead have no bones, I thought. They fall over like sacks of flour.

The war went on. The Germans had dug in north of Belgrade, on the other side of the Rivers Sava and Danube. The Russians had left the fighting to the Yugoslavs, while they advanced north toward Hungary. All able men were conscripted, and the fighting was fierce. Belgrade was a city of the wounded. One saw people on crutches on every corner. They walked slowly, at times carrying mess kits with their daily ration. There were soup kitchens where such people got their meals.

Once, chased by a friend, I rounded the corner of my street at top speed and collided with one of these invalids, spilling his soup on the sidewalk. I won't forget the look he gave me. "Oh child," he said softly. I was too stunned to speak. I didn't even have the sense to pick up his crutch. I watched him do it himself with great difficulty.

Around that time we heard that my mother's brother was wounded too. His story is absolutely incredible—as I found out later. He first fought with the Royalists, was captured by the Communists, lined up against the wall to be shot, and pardoned on the spot with the option that he join them. He did. The last few months of the war he fought with the Communists.

This is how he got wounded. The Germans surrounded him and two other soldiers in a farmhouse. They drew lots to see who would try to break out first. My uncle was last. The first man, after much hesitation, took off, only to be cut down by the Germans. The same thing happened to the second one, although he managed to run a good distance toward the woods. My uncle had no choice but to follow. At some point while running, he felt great warmth. It was winter; the ground was covered with snow. Then he passed out.

When he came to, he was lying naked and barefoot in the farmhouse with most of his stuff stolen and a wound high up inside one of his thighs. He got up and stumbled out, shortly afterward reaching a road where, eventually—it's hard for him to say how much time had elapsed—an old man came by in a horse cart, threw him a blanket, and took him along. All of a sudden—I still don't believe this—the old man was killed. A stray bullet hit him, and he fell over backwards where my uncle sat huddled. Luckily, the horses kept going, so eventually they reached some Russians, who took him to a medical unit where he was revived.

Now the tragic farce really begins. The Russians in those days had a cure-all for every serious leg wound: amputate the leg. That's what they told my uncle they were going to do. He was very unhappy, crying even, while the doctor cheerfully reminded him that he still had one leg left. Anyway, they strapped him to the field operating table and got ready to cut the leg, when all hell broke loose. Grenades, bombs flying. The tent collapsed. Everybody ran out, leaving him there. When the shooting was over, they came back but were no longer in the mood for the operation. He ended up, somehow, on a farm, where he was exceptionally well nursed by the kind people who lived there, and so on. End of that story.

By the time my brother was born, and he and my mother had

come home from the clinic, I was in the business of selling gunpowder. It worked this way. Many of us kids had stashes of ammunition, which we collected during the street fighting. The gunpowder from these rounds was sold to the older kids, who, so I heard, were in turn selling it to the fishermen on the Danube. This last part I cannot guarantee. *Selling* is always the wrong word. We traded gunpowder for old comic books, toys, cans of food, and God knows what else. I remember a particular tasty can of American corned beef that I devoured all by myself, sitting in the winter sunlight behind the great Byzantine church of St. Mark.

I have no idea how long this went on. I had a large laundry basket full of rounds of ammunition hidden in the cellar. Removing the gunpowder was done in the following way: one stuck the bullet part into the kitchen spigot and yanked the shell sideways until it came off. Absolute secrecy was, of course, required. My mother had no idea how I spent my time, although she was puzzled by some of the nice-looking toys I suddenly owned. But she was busy with the new baby, and I was already an expert liar. Then one day a kid on our block lost both of his hands. He was trying to remove the long black sticks of gunpowder from some sort of artillery shell. That's what he told me later, while I tried to avoid looking at his two newly healed and still red stumps.

I started school in the spring of 1945, but I don't remember much about it. My parents taught me how to read early on, and I breezed through the first few grades. The classes that spring were sporadic. My interests, in any case, were elsewhere. The streets were full of semi-abandoned children. Gangs were being formed. Legendary hoods held whole neighborhoods in terror. One couldn't walk to school by the most direct route. There were enemies everywhere just waiting for someone like me to walk down their block.

We went in packs everywhere, but sometimes there was no choice and I had to go alone. I knew every backyard in my section of the city through which one could wind one's way unobserved. Still, a few times I got caught and beaten. For no reason. Just because I was from another neighborhood. The idea was not to cry, since seeing you cry made them ecstatic. I know, because we did the same thing to the kids from other neighborhoods we seized on our street.

When you're little you can't fight very well, so you'd better be quick on your feet. Luckily, I was—which was just as well, since someone was always trying to beat me up. An older boy in our neighborhood really had it in for me. This is what happened: he and a couple of other guys were going to the movies, and he had this can of beef—or whatever it was—which he wanted me to keep for him. No problem. I was happy to oblige. So off they went. A bit later the rest of us decided to play soccer on the street, so I decided to hide the can. I went into our building, made sure no one was following me, then descended toward the back, where the entrance to the cellar was and where there was a pile of old furniture and some kind of large barrel in one of the corners, and placed the can of beef carefully behind the barrel. After again making sure that no one was watching me, I rejoined my friends on the street to play soccer.

Hours later the owner of the can returned from the movies and asked me for it. I ran off to fetch it. When I got down there, when I reached behind the barrel in the dark, I discovered to my horror that the can wasn't there anymore. I couldn't believe it! It was impossible! I moved the furniture away from the wall and even the heavy barrel, and still—nothing! A complete mystery, as I tried to tell its owner, who was waiting impatiently outside. He didn't believe me, of course. He started punching me then and there, while I protested my innocence.

As for the can, I never found out who swiped it and how. For years I'd think about it, visualizing every detail, remembering my caution and deliberateness, even down to the sound the can made as I placed it on the concrete floor. The best explanation is that one of my friends had followed me, but, even if one did and was the culprit, he would have told me about it years later, since I brought the subject up often, to everyone's amusement: The Mystery of Simic's Disappearing Can of American Army Beef. They all thought I had eaten it.

My mother had much to worry about. There was no news of my father. Unknown to us, he had reached Italy and was promptly arrested by the Germans, who accused him of being a spy. He was in prison in Milan for a few months when the Americans liberated him. He had no desire to return to Belgrade. He didn't like the Communists, and he didn't get along with my mother. Before the war he had worked for an American company, had many American business connections, and had always wanted to see that country.

There were plenty of other reasons to be concerned. The Communists were firmly in power. People were being arrested left and right. Everybody was afraid. In school there was indoctrination.

I remember a young man coming to talk to us about communism. The subject of religion came up. He said that there was no God and asked if some of us still believed in God. We all kept our mouths shut except for one scrawny little kid, who said he did. The fellow asked the kid, what could God do? Everything, the kid said. Well, the fellow said, if you were to ask him to help you pick up this table, would he do it? "I wouldn't ask him," said the kid, eyeing the heavy table. "Why not?" insisted the man. "It'd be a dumb thing to ask for," replied the kid, barely audible.

That ended that. But there were more sinister things. One day the same young man asked if our parents at home complained about the new regime. No one said anything this time. When I told my mother what happened, she informed me, in no uncertain terms, that she would kill me if I ever opened my mouth. In any case, she did not take any chances. Anytime I walked into a room, the grown-ups would shut up and eye me suspiciously. I had plenty to be guilty about, and it must have shown on my face, for there would be a long cross-examination: "What did you tell them?" "Nothing! I swear it!" And so it went.

My life on the street was also getting more complicated. I hung around with the older boys. There was stealing. We stole for profit and for the fun of it—anything we could get our hands on that looked remotely valuable. I was usually the one to make the snatch, since I was the smallest and the fastest. I remember being chased by an ax-wielding man whose bicycle pump I had taken from his yard while he had his back turned. I remember walking into a grocery store, grabbing something from the counter, and running away. This was for practice. There was not much to be found in those stores. Most of the food was rationed. If you took someone's monthly ration of sugar, you were committing an unforgivable crime.

Which reminds me. There were people who kept chickens and even pigs in their apartments if they could get them. I assume they were afraid to keep them in the backyard. They'd have to keep guard around the clock. There might have even been a law against it.

So, it was a secret. There'd be a rumor that so and so is keeping a pig in his bathroom. Supposedly, as the pig grew, they would give it the living room, and they themselves would move into the bathroom. That was the rumor anyway.

My mother was scandalized. The apartment on which the suspicion fell had previously belonged to a piano teacher. Now some hicks lived in it, but the piano was still there. My mother kept worrying about the piano, seeing the pig sleeping under it or scratching its back against one of the legs. Pretty funny, I thought.

But then it wasn't. When my friends heard about it, they figured we should steal the pig. I was supposed to climb on the third-floor balcony when the people were at work, open the front door, and let the gang in and the pig out. Even more than the climb, the idea of meeting the pig terrified me. I imagined it to be huge. A monstrous hog with its hump reaching to the ceiling. Who knows what would have really happened if we had not gone on a trip just then.

My mother had heard that my father was alive and well in Trieste. She was determined that we should join him immediately. The frontier between Yugoslavia and Italy was still open, since the two countries disputed the area around Trieste. There was a chance we could slip across, but it was dangerous. One could get arrested. One could get shot, too, of course. My mother had no illusions about that. Still, she felt she had to try.

We left Belgrade for the coast in the fall of 1945. The train journey took forever. The tracks were still in terrible shape. All along the way one could see derailed trains and bombed-out stations. There were soldiers everywhere and tremendous crowds of people trying to get on the train. Although the Germans were gone, people could still feel their presence. We were Serbs in

Croatia, where Croatian Fascists spent the war exterminating Serbs. We didn't open our mouths much.

This was the train my father took, I kept thinking. What I was seeing now, he saw. That cluster of trees, for example. Or that house high on a hill! In Zagreb we spent the night in a hotel. I remember the dark, poorly lit streets. They were empty. It was late. Our room was small and cold. Everything looked different. It was no longer the same country.

The next day, when we reached Opatia-Fiume, that once fashionable Austro-Hungarian sea resort, we heard that the border was closed. Still, if one knew the right people, one could cross illegally. So we stayed.

It was a big, old seaside hotel with high, ornate ceilings, crystal chandeliers, and mirrors everywhere. We took our meals in a large, immaculately set, and almost empty dining room, which looked out at the gray sea. I've wondered since who the few other guests were. They had a secretive air about them, didn't speak to each other, and rarely acknowledged our nods. I could walk for hours along the long hallways without meeting anyone or hearing a sound. Once I did hear sobs, muffled sobs, and even got my eye to the keyhole but could see nothing. There was just the gray sea through the open balcony door and the silence of the hotel around me. The woman had stopped crying.

We went back to Belgrade, but my mother was stubborn. She found someone who knew a reliable person who, for a price, could take us across the border into Austria. I was told nothing. I was under the impression that we were going to spend our summer vacation in the mountains of Slovenia. Again, we found ourselves in an elegant, half-empty chalet, sleeping late and taking long mountain walks.

One evening we walked farther than was our custom. We sat on a couple of rocks in the woods, and my mother told me that this was the night we'd be going to my father.

It was almost pitch-dark when a man came to take us to a farmhouse, where two armed men waited. The rest of the night we spent climbing the mountains, with my mother carrying my infant brother in her arms. They had given him something so he would sleep. We had to be absolutely quiet, even when we took brief rests.

We couldn't see much for most of the way. The moon only came out when we crossed the border in the wee hours. We were on the side of a hill, and Yugoslavia was down below. We sat on the grass and had our first talk of the night, and the men smoked. This was a mistake, as it turned out. We heard someone shout something in German. One of our guides leapt to his feet and opened fire, and the two of them took off in the direction of Yugoslavia, leaving us alone. After a long while there was another shout in German. This time my mother replied, and soon enough they came out of the trees. We were in the hands of the American-Austrian border patrol, and that cheered us up tremendously.

The Americans took us to their barracks, where we spent the rest of the night. In the morning I had my first sight of the American army. Some of the soldiers were black, which fascinated me. Everybody was very friendly, giving us chewing gum and chocolate. We ate in the mess hall with everyone else, a big breakfast of eggs and bacon. There was even cocoa! My mother was happier than I have ever seen her. This was paradise.

Our problems started when the Americans handed us over to the English army, whose zone of occupation this was. A colonel sternly asked my mother for our passports. My mother laughed. After our all-night mountain hike our clothes were in tatters, and our hands and faces were covered with scratches. My mother then tried a bit of humor. She told him, in the best English she could summon, that if we had our passports we would have surely taken a sleeping car. The fellow was not amused. All her explanations fell on deaf ears. What he did then—and it came to us as a big surprise and horror—is to drive us to the border and hand us over to the Yugoslav border guards. He saluted, they saluted, and we were back in Yugoslavia and under arrest.

We didn't know, of course, that this kind of thing happened often. The English were sending back Russian POWs and anybody else from Eastern Europe they got their hands on. People begged, threw their children off the trains, committed suicide. The English didn't care what happened. Their pal Stalin packed everybody off to the labor camps, where, of course, many perished.

Our case was not so tragic. We were transported from prison to prison for the next two weeks, until we reached Belgrade. Some of it was rather idyllic—like being escorted on foot through the gorgeous Slovenian countryside and stopping by some roadside orchard to eat apples together with our guard. At other times the cells were crowded, and there were some nasty-looking characters. I remember one tall old man who was supposed to have killed several people. He just stood in the middle of the cell, all day, with his eyes closed. Nobody dared come near him or speak above a whisper.

In Belgrade my brother and I were released into the hands of my grandmother, and my mother was kept in prison for another four months. Her defense was that she simply wanted to be with her husband and was not given the legal means to do so. This was true enough, although probably not the reason why they let her go with such little fuss. The jails at that time were full of people with more interesting political transgressions. We were small fry. They slapped my mother a few times, once right in front of us, but that was all.

As for me, I thoroughly enjoyed being in jail. A couple of times they put me in with the men. This was hard on my mother because she worried that we'd get separated and she would not see me again. The cell doors would open at some ungodly night hour, when they take people to be interrogated, and this little kid would be pushed in. The prisoners were stunned. The cells were packed. They'd have to make room for me, make sure I had plenty of covers. They also wanted to hear my story. I obliged, of course. The bedbugs made it hard to sleep. I embroidered, how I embroidered! I was at the center of attention. At home, too, all the relatives and friends were waiting to hear what happened. I reenacted the gunfight and the beatings of my mother for the benefit of all those grim and weary faces, night after night, inventing more and more fantastic details, until eventually they began to laugh at me, and I stopped.

4

My childhood is a black-and-white movie. O rainy evenings, dimly lit streets! My mother is leading me by the hand into the gloomy cinema where the performance has already started; where a boy is running down a country road under a sky full of ominous-looking clouds; where he kneels on someone's grave pulling weeds while the wind howls among the crosses and bare trees; where later he visits a strange old woman, who sits in her wedding dress at the table full of moldy, cobweb-covered food. Mice run in and out of the huge wedding cake. Best of all, there's a beautiful girl who teases him cruelly, whom he gets to kiss once on the dark staircase.

It's the dark ages I'm describing now, things that happened fifty years ago. My memory is so poor that everything appears poorly lit and full of shadows. Even the beautiful summer mornings lack the brightness they undoubtedly had. And the nights . . . they are as thick as dreams from which one awakes troubled yet unable to remember anything specific. Is this how it is with everybody?

Writing brings it back. There's the logic of chronology, which forces one to think about what comes next. There's also the logic of the imagination. One image provokes another without rhyme or reason—perhaps with plenty of hidden rhyme and reason! I have to believe that. Otherwise, how do I explain why that movie has reminded me of a score of other things?

In those far-off days women mended stockings in the evening. To have a "run" in one's stocking was catastrophic. Stockings were expensive, and so was electricity. We would all sit around the table with a single lamp, my grandmother reading the papers, we children pretending to do our homework while watching my mother spreading her red-painted fingernails inside the transparent stocking.

Mother told us how when she was a child she heard a man plead for his life. She remembered the stars, the dark shape of trees along the road on which they were fleeing the Austrian army in World War I in a slow-moving oxcart. "That man sounded terribly frightened out there in the woods," she said. Afterward, all they could hear were the wheels of the cart straining and gasping with each turn.

I shared the solitude of my childhood with a black cat. I sat by the window for hours on end watching the empty street, while she sat on the bed washing herself. When night fell, I stretched on the bed, and she watched the street.

Round about midnight, the phone across the street would ring a long time, but no one would come to answer it. After that the cat's tail would flicker a long time until it put me to sleep.

On rainy days I played chess with the cat, which pretended to doze. Once, when my mother turned on the table lamp, the silhouettes of the few remaining chess figures could be seen clearly on the wall grown very large. I was afraid to move. I didn't even dare to take a breath.

When I finally did, the cat had vanished, taking the chess set with it and leaving me as I was in the same mean little room with its one window and its view of the empty street.

There was a maid in our house who let me put my hand under her skirt. I was five or six years old. I remember the dampness of her crotch and my surprise that there was all that hair down there. I couldn't get enough of it. She would crawl under the table where I had my military fort and my toy soldiers. I don't remember what was said, if anything. Just her hand, firmly guiding my fingers to that spot.

Here's another early memory: a baby carriage pushed by a humpbacked old woman, her son sitting in it, both legs amputated.

She was haggling with the greengrocer when the carriage got away from her. The street was steep, so it rolled downhill with the cripple waving his crutch as if urging it on faster and faster; his mother screaming for help, and everybody else was laughing as if they were watching a funny movie . . . Keystone cops about to go over a cliff . . .

They laughed because they knew it would end well in the movies. They were surprised when it didn't in life.

Years later, in the biography of the Russian poet Marina Tsvetaeva, I read that her first poetry reading in Paris took place on February 6, 1925, and the newspaper accounts mention that there were also three musicians on the program—Madame Cunelli, who sang old Italian songs, Professor Mogilewski, who played violin, and V. E. Byutsov, who was on piano. This was astonishing to me. Madame Cunelli, whose first name was Nina, was a friend of my mother's. They had both studied with the same voice teacher, Madame Kedrov, in Paris, and then some-how Nina Cunelli ended up in Belgrade during World War II, where she taught me Russian and French songs when she came to visit my mother, songs that I still know well. I remember that she was a beautiful woman, a little older than my mother, and that she went somewhere abroad after the war ended.

I did not tell you how I got lice wearing a German helmet. This used to be a famous story in my family. Every time the kinfolk got together, sooner or later, it was inevitable, someone would bring up my German helmet full of lice. Everybody thought this was the funniest thing they had ever heard. Old people had tears of laughter in their eyes. This child was dumb enough to walk around the neighborhood with a German helmet full of lice. They were crawling all over it. Any fool could see them.

I sat there saying nothing, pretending to be equally amused, nodding my head while thinking to myself, what a bunch of idiots. They had no idea what I went through to get that helmet, and I wasn't about to tell them.

The day after the liberation of Belgrade, I was up in the old cemetery with a few friends, kind of snooping around with no particular purpose in mind. Then, all of a sudden, we saw them! A couple of German soldiers, obviously dead, stretched out on the ground. We drew closer to take a better look. They had no weapons, their boots were gone, but there was a helmet that had fallen to the side of one of them. I don't remember what the others took, but I went for the helmet on tiptoes, as if not to wake the dead man. I also kept my eyes averted. I never saw his face, even if sometimes I think I did. Everything else about that moment is still intensely clear to me.

5

He was the meanest-looking street punk I ever laid my eyes on. They called him Singa, because he clearly belonged in Sing Sing prison, although, him being in Belgrade and in Communist Yugoslavia at that, the chances of him ending up on the shores of the gray Hudson were slim. He was just an overgrown sixteen-year-old boy, but the evil attributed to him and the even worse evil he was capable of at the slightest provocation made him seem much bigger and much tougher than he actually was. Where he lived, what crimes he actually committed, and what eventually happened to him, I do not know. I only remember he once came to sit on the steps of my grade school just as classes were about to start. He sat on the bottom, obviously in a foul mood, and no one dared pass him to enter the school. Hundreds of us stood on the other side of the street watching him. The rumor was that he'd let you go in providing you allowed him to rap your head once with his knuckles. Some kid, worried about being late for school, took up the challenge and ran into the building wailing and holding his head. The rest of us just looked at each other with disbelief, while Singa lit himself a cigarette. At that point, out of the school came our muscle-bound gym teacher. He stood at the top of the stairs and ordered Singa to clear out immediately before the police were called. He even shook his fist a little. Singa took time to acknowledge him. Finally, he spat in his direction. Like everything else about him, that gob of spit was superhuman. It traveled an impossible distance with astonishing accuracy. It hit the creased, tan trousers of the gym teacher right at the crotch, making it look as if he had just let out a little pee out of fright. He made a quick retreat after he heard us laugh. There were whoops and hollers, while Singa flicked cigarette ashes, not deigning to look at us.

It was then that I experienced what could turn out to be the most triumphant moment in my life. There was a boy in my neighborhood, a school dropout and a close friend of mine, who happened to come by. He asked what was going on, saw me in the crowd, saw Singa sitting there, and motioned to me to come over. I didn't know what he had in mind, and I was reluctant to come near the monster. It turned out, his brother and Singa's brother were pals, and they knew each other, so that there was nothing to worry about. I any case, I found myself standing right next to Singa. While my friend explained that I was okay, Singa eyed me suspiciously, as if making up his mind. He didn't say anything; he just turned his head away, and I mounted the steps. It was when I reached the top and was about to run and open the glass door beyond which the teachers cowered that I remembered to turn around and face the crowd below. In their admiring and envious eyes I saw my glory. Even the girls who had never paid any attention to me before seemed to be positively in awe. I stood and watched them from that height much longer than it was prudent with Singa close by, and I turned and walked in, our ancient history teacher even shuffling over to hold the door open for me.

6

When my grandfather was dying from diabetes, when he had already one leg cut off at the knee and they were threatening to do the same to the other, his old buddy Savo Lozanic used to pay him a visit every morning to keep him company. The two would reminisce about this and that and even have a few laughs.

One morning my grandmother had to leave him alone in the house, as she had to attend the funeral of a relative. That's what gave him the idea. He hopped out of bed and into the kitchen, where he found candles and matches. He got back into the bed, somehow placed one candle above his head and the other at his feet, and lit them. Finally, he pulled the sheet over his face and began to wait.

When his friend knocked, there was no answer. The door being unlocked, he went in, calling out from time to time. The kitchen was empty. A fat gray cat slept on the dining room table. When he entered the bedroom and saw the bed with the sheet and lit candles, he let out a wail and then broke into sobs as he groped for a chair to sit down.

"Shut up, Savo," my grandfather said sternly from under his sheet. "Can't you see I'm just practicing."

One night we went to see a performance of a great Hungarian hypnotist. It took place in the big hotel ballroom at Lake Bled in Slovenia. The place was packed but also strangely silent. You know how it is with hypnotists—they are liable to call on you, bring you up on the stage, and make you do strange things. This man had a reputation for doing wonders. And he looked the part: black tuxedo, black hair slicked down, bushy eyebrows, terrifying eyes, a commanding voice. He made my mother guess what was in people's pockets. She sat on the stage with her eyes closed, while he stood in the audience pointing at someone. She spoke slowly and in a hoarse whisper. The audience gasped and then applauded.

I don't really remember this very well, though I will never forget how my mother's voice sounded. There was another person underneath the familiar one. A complete stranger I had to be wary of from now on.

The next morning in the hotel dining room we were seated at the same table with the hypnotist at breakfast. It was simple. There were three of us, he was alone, and there was not another empty chair in the place.

"Don't look at him," my mother whispered in my ear, giving me a kick under the table to emphasize the point. The great hypnotist had no interest in us. I don't think he even recognized my mother from the night before. He ate his breakfast staring into his plate and chewing slowly. Even I could tell he had false teeth. He was a very old man. When he held the butter knife, his hand trembled. We were done first and left the table without looking back.

There was a time in 1947 or 1948 when we had almost nothing to eat. My mother didn't have her job at the conservatory back yet, and we had great difficulties making ends meet. I remember coming home from school one afternoon, telling her I was hungry, and watching her burst into tears. The only eatable thing we had in the house that day were some onions, which I chopped. There was no oil, just some stale bread and salt. I remember thinking, this tastes pretty good.

My mother, who is an awful cook under any circumstances, used to make a kind of meatless stew, consisting of potatoes, onions, and perhaps a few carrots. This is what we ate all the time. By the third day, after all the reheating, the dish tasted foul. I'd gag at every mouthful and would have to drink big gulps of water in between to get it down. The bread was rationed. There would be a large slice of black bread, which I always ate last, as a dessert.

The kids on my street talked about food all the time. Someone, for example, would describe in great detail salami he once ate. We listened, interrupting the narrative from time to time to ask for clarifications about various nuances of taste. Someone else opined about the advantages and disadvantages of fried versus roasted chicken. Others liked sweets. They rhapsodized about ice cream, Swiss chocolate, different kinds of cakes and pies. My own reverie was almost always about pigs' ears. In my opinion there was nothing tastier than a roasted suckling pig's ear. There was a story about that.

When the holidays came, everybody feasted. Belgrade is surrounded by farming country, and if one knew the right people one could get just about any kind of meat—for a price. A fat peasant woman would come to see us on the sly and, after bargaining with my mother, would raise her skirts to reveal long strips of bacon wrapped around her waist.

Since we didn't have any money, we'd barter. A pair of my father's black patent leather dancing shoes went for a chicken. Sometimes the yokels could not make up their minds about what they wanted in exchange, so we'd let them look around. They'd walk from room to room with us in tow, looking things over, shaking their heads when we suggested a particular item. They were hard to please. Carpets, clocks, armchairs, and fancy pottery were exchanged for various yard animals over the years.

Everybody did that. The sidewalks were covered with roasted suckling pigs on Christmas day. All sizes of pigs in all kinds of roasting pans. People brought them to the bakeries where, for a small charge, they'd be roasted properly in the big oven. By late morning there was no more room on the counters, so they had to put the done pigs out until the owners came to collect them.

The sight of them is still clear to me, but I have no idea what year this was. It had started to snow, so one of the baker's helpers was trying to cover the roasted pigs with newspapers. The paper would get greasy immediately and wet. It was not easy to cover the ears. They were cocked as if trying to make out the voices of their owners. There was a lot of milling around and jabbering while looking for the right pan. Everybody was in a good mood. The pigs with apples in their mouths looked eager to be eaten.

Ours certainly did. I had to carry it several blocks over the slippery sidewalk. The pan was heavy and full of grease, which I didn't want to spill, so I steered carefully, one step at a time.

Suddenly, there was a gust of wind. The newspaper fluttered and flew in my face. It made me tip the pan. The pig slid against my chest, and I was covered with grease. There was quite a scene when I got home.

Dogs followed me around for days. My mother tried to clean the stain on my winter overcoat as best as she could, but the smell remained. On cold nights I'd throw the overcoat over my blanket, sniff the roast, and see those smiling pigs on the sidewalk.

It is raining. It is Sunday. A gray afternoon in the late fall. My radio is turned down low. I am on the bed reading. Time has stopped. I have a deep sense of well-being. I love the rain even though it prevents me from going out to play.

I no longer remember the name of the book or what year this was, but such moments with books are among my happiest memories. I started reading at an early age, because my father had a large library. There were books even in my room. They made me curious. First I turned their pages searching for pictures, and then I looked at the words until with my parents' help I did learn how to read. By the time I was ten I was in love with books.

My friends read too. We liked cowboy stories, mysteries, sea adventures, and comic books, of course. Most of these books were published before the war, and their supply was limited. It was possible, and this eventually happened to me, to have read all the books available in our circle. They could not be purchased in stores or taken out of libraries. They were passed down from our elders, and then we shared them among us.

There were long periods, however, when there was nothing new to read. I had to turn to my father's library. I read Zola, Dickens, and even a little of Dostoyevsky out of sheer boredom. Then I was hooked. *Oliver Twist* I liked very much; *Great Expectations* was even more wonderful. Thomas Mann's *Magic Mountain* was impossible to read. I loved the Serbian epic ballads and folk poems, but other poetry mostly left me cold.

That need to read has never left me. I still read all kinds of books on all kinds of subjects. Consequently, I know a little about a great many things. I could live and die in a good library, and I don't have an inordinate respect for great learning. I'm suspicious of the pedantry that kind of learning is prone to. Still, it seems incredible that one would not want to know what is inside every book in the world.

Reading and imagining; traveling to far away places and making up other lives and identities for oneself. So many places, so many lives! Who would not want to relive again those sweet hours of reverie when a good book got hold of one's imagination?

Then there was music. My radio was always on. I discovered American jazz and could not get enough of it. Late at night the radio would pick up the U.S. army stations in Germany and Austria. This is the world I want to be a part of, it occurred to me. The world of Duke Ellington's "Mood Indigo," Count Basie's "Lester Leaps In," and Billie Holiday singing "Mean to Me."

During the day my mother, who was a voice teacher, an opera singing teacher, often had her conservatory students over to the house for the lessons. I knew, by the age of five, most of the major operatic arias. I even sang them to myself as I played with my toys, which gave Mother the idea that I was destined to become a great musician or a conductor. The outcome was terrible. I had two years of violin lessons followed by two years of piano, and they were pure torture as far as I was concerned.

The world was going up in flames, and I was practicing violin. The snot-nosed Nero sawing away . . . It wasn't just the instrument that gave me trouble but the carrying case, too. I never saw another one like it. It was made of wood, and it was big and heavy. The handle was on top instead of on the side, as was customary. It was made of brass, and there were brass ornaments on the box. "It looks like a baby coffin," concluded one of my friends after examining it. He was right. Everyone who saw it thought the same thing. People stared and shook their heads when I came puffing down the street.

My teacher lived on the other side of town, so I had a long trek carrying that thing. To make myself even more ridiculous I wore a cousin's overcoat that reached down to my feet. I looked like a little old man. My teacher's apartment was always cold. The room where we had our lesson was large and almost empty of furniture. She would say nothing until the first few scratchy notes of my violin, then her eyes would fill with horror, and she would start shouting. I was terrified of that old woman. I also loved her because after a good scolding she would give me something to eat. Something rare and exotic like a chocolate filled with sweet liqueur. We'd sit in that big, empty room, and she'd watch me eat. "Poor child," she'd say, and I thought it had something to do with my not practicing enough, my being dim-witted when she tried to explain what I was doing wrong on the instrument, but today I have a feeling that's not what she meant. In fact, I suspect she had something entirely different in mind. That is why I'm writing this memoir: to find out what it was.

This all ended when my brother jumped on the violin, which I had "carelessly" left on the bed. That was my version. The truth is far more perverse. I saw him jumping on the bed, bouncing himself off the way one does off a trampoline. He did that all the time. One day I got the idea. I slid the violin under one of the blankets. It splintered into hundreds of pieces when he landed on it with his full weight. I had to pretend I was grief-stricken, terribly upset, and so forth. Still, I don't think I completely fooled them. Violins were very expensive, and my mother realized by then that my heart was not in it. So, there was no mention of me getting another one.

Still, I liked classical music well enough. Mother took me to a lot of concerts and opera performances. If her students were not around singing, she'd be practicing scales herself. When my father was around, he sang, too. Operatic arias, folks songs, Gypsy songs, Russian ones—someone was always singing. She even sang folk songs on the radio. I thought she was terrible. Too middle-class and her voice too cultivated to sing the hick songs right—the way my father knew how to do after a couple of bottles of wine. As it happens, he too had at one time studied singing at the conservatory. They even gave a couple of concerts together in the early days, sang Mozart duets.

"Your father was not serious," mother told me over and over as I was growing up. She said he spent all his time in the taverns singing and raising hell. A good-hearted man but totally unreli-able as a husband, according to her. He'd step out for a beer and be gone for two days. The first time it happened, she went out of her mind with worry and anger, but then she kind of got used to it. He'd get so drunk he would have to literally crawl home on all fours. In his expensive suit, his fine Italian hat, and English shoes—what a sight! All the neighbors would stick their heads out of their windows and enjoy themselves. "There goes George Simic crawling back to his wife," someone would shout, and they'd all laugh. I did, too, on hearing the story, which infuriated my mother. "You'll end up like your father," was her opinion.

Or, even worse, I could very well end up like one of my father's brothers. There were three of them, and as far as my mother was concerned only the youngest, Boris, who wanted to become an opera singer, was okay. The oldest one, Mosha, was a felon pure and simple. The middle one, Mladen, was, despite his charm, basically a crook. His two sisters were snotty bitches. My father's father was a nasty old man and my grandmother an illiterate, superstitious peasant woman.

All this meant that I hardly ever saw my father's family. Whenever I paid them a visit, I went alone with plenty of warning not to listen to what they say. My grandfather, for example, liked to blaspheme and make unpatriotic remarks. He made fun of priests, politicians, Serbian national heroes—everything everybody held sacred. I loved to listen to him. He made me laugh, and my grandmother made me stuff myself with delicious food. Even he, however, had a warning for me about Mosha. He threw him out of the house when he was still in grade school. This was hard to believe, but everybody assured me that it was true. Mosha was a bad man, but the stories my grandfather told me about him were very funny.

Mosha once had a job driving a streetcar on the line that went past my grandfather's house. If he saw any member of the family waiting at the stop, he would drive right by shaking his fist. Luckily, he did not last long on that job. One night after the streetcars stopped running, he took his girlfriend for a ride through the dark, sleepy streets of Belgrade. They cruised at top speed with him clanging the bell continuously. The whole city woke up. He was fired.

I met Mosha for the first time when I was twelve years old. He had just come out of the prison. As the Russians and Yugoslav Communists were liberating Belgrade from Germans, he, who had never had any political interests whatsoever, proclaimed himself a royalist in some dive on the outskirts. Not a wise thing to do under the circumstances. In any case, he was inquiring about the news of my father. A tall, handsome man in an elegant gray winter overcoat who addressed my mother and me with great politeness. Not at all what I had been led to believe.

My mother's family was very different. They were what you call "respectable." They lived in apartments cluttered with fine old furniture, oil paintings, and thick Persian carpets. They never used bad language. When there was something the children were not supposed to understand, they spoke French among themselves. They lived in fear, constant fear of everything. If I happened to sneeze, my grandmother would immediately put me to bed. "Oh my God! Oh my God," she'd go wringing her hands as if I had already died. She had buried three of her six children; she had plenty of reason to expect the worst.

Still, it made the life around her constraining. She lived one floor below us, took care of my brother and me while my mother worked, and often cooked for us. I had a genuine love for her. She was kind, and she could show affection much more than my mother ever could. At the same time, she was unhappy. Her life had been miserable. She married a young officer who gambled away most of her money, gave her six children, and then retired at the age of forty to his native village. She struggled financially and kept up appearances. My grandfather made occasional visits to Belgrade, but for all practical purposes they lived apart. There was resentment in the air and deep melancholy.

In the meantime, I was in big trouble. Without anyone knowing, I had stopped going to school. The school that I attended and liked one day turned me away. Unknown to my mother and me, they had changed school districts, and the day I arrived to begin my sixth grade they told me that I was now supposed to go to another school on the other side of town. When I presented myself there the next day, they had no record of my transfer. I was advised to stay home for the next three days and return on Monday, by which time my file should have arrived and I could be properly registered. Well, I never went back. At first I only wanted to prolong my summer vacation. I kept postponing the day of my return, so that weeks went by until it became impossible to go back. My mother knew nothing about this. I'd leave every morning for school and return with the rest of the neighborhood children in the afternoon. It was the middle of January when somebody finally figured out that I was unaccounted for and sent the cops after me.

While the weather was still balmy, it was rather pleasant to roam the streets and parks of Belgrade, but then the rains came and the cold weather. If I were lucky and had managed to steal some money from my mother's purse, I went to the movies. Otherwise, I shivered in doorways. The cold, clear days were better. I traversed the city from one end to the other to keep warm, and the hours passed quickly. Couple of times I was so preoccupied with my thoughts and worries, I walked past the outskirts where the countryside began. I remember one such terrifying moment, turning around and seeing the city in the distance.

The movies also had their terrors. These were shabby, old movie palaces with rat-eaten red velvet curtains and creaky wooden seats. They were cold and drafty in the morning. The customers were other school dropouts, university students, and tired-looking people who must've worked the night shift. They'd fall asleep immediately and wake in the middle of the film, their faces wild-eyed with incomprehension.

Often I, too, had no idea what was going on, although I paid close attention. Some of these movies were ancient. It was hard to know whether the weather was always foul or the film was so old and grainy it only looked that way. The people on the screen spoke French or English, and the subtitles were either faded or they did not make much sense. After a while I'd give up reading them and just watch. There was always some beautiful woman to follow around and commit her every expression to memory. Otherwise, as far as I was concerned, nothing much happened in these films. People sat around talking interminably in their living rooms. How I longed to see them on a train or, even better, on an ocean liner. At times there were glimpses of strange cities. Streets full of people rushing off somewhere.

Some were black, and some were even Chinese. I saw a school that terrified me. Places where orphans were sent a hundred years ago and where they beat you with a stick. I spent hours going over these scenes in my mind, inserting myself in the life of its heroes and sharing their adventures.

7

From its title, *The Bicycle Thief,* which forewarns us that a bike will be stolen, everything is inevitable in this film. "To hell with poverty," says the man who has gotten a job after two years of waiting. His bike will be stolen, and finding it will be like looking for a needle in a haystack. "We find it or we don't eat," says the man to his son, and there's your plot, with a weight of inevitability worthy of Greek tragedy.

The fellow in a shabby suit and the streets and buildings of Rome all looked familiar. There are parts of all large European cities that are almost identical in architecture. My childhood took place among such late-nineteenth-century apartment houses and office buildings in downtown Belgrade. After the war they were gray and rundown, their walls peeling.

I first saw *The Bicycle Thief* in the late 1940s. Ordinarily, I cared only for American films, westerns especially, but they were rarely imported in the glory days of Stalinism. We mostly saw Soviet films and a few so-called progressive French and Italian ones. The sad thing about socialist realism in the arts is that even a child of ten finds its idealized characters and wholesome message hopelessly boring and fake. I went to see De Sica's film with considerable suspicion and was surprised to be so deeply moved.

Like the people in the film, most of the families I knew were poor and unemployed and had little to eat. Both the young and the old in our neighborhood stole. I once entered a bakery, took a chunk of bread from the counter, and ran out with customers in pursuit. For years afterward, there were neighbors who continued to accuse me of swiping, on different occasions, a garden hose, an ax, and a baby carriage and were astonished that I continued to deny it. A movie about stealing a bicycle was something I understood perfectly even at that early age.

I recollect little of that first viewing of the film except for a few scenes that have remained vivid: the father and the boy after a day of looking for the stolen bike decide to splurge with whatever little money they had and have a meal in a trattoria. There's a rich kid at the next table, eating carefully with a fork and knife in the company of his family, who keeps turning and watching Bruno gobble his food. He wears the same clothes boys of that social class used to wear even in postwar Communist Belgrade. We'd see one of them on the street in a sailor suit holding the hand of his mother. They always went around with their mothers; otherwise, they would have been beaten up. In the meantime, there'd be a lot of rubbernecking back and forth just as in the movie.

I also remember the bedsheets the Ricci's pawn to get the bicycle out of hock. There are shelves and shelves packed with old bedsheets. A man climbs the shelves like a monkey to add the new bundle. Thousands of bedsheets on which people slept and made love. More used bedsheets than anyone ever saw. That scene took my breath away every time I viewed the movie.

I caught the film several more times over the years, and each time I had the same thought: this is the grainy black-and-white look of my childhood. The streetcar early Sunday morning, for instance, when they accompany the trash collectors on their rounds. Or the thieves' market in the rain. Or the horse's head bowing down framed in the door of the trattoria. The musicians inside remind me of Italian prisoners of war who came to our door begging for food. The whole movie is like that. The way a poor city kid sees the world.

You don't need Hamlet and Lear or an assassination of a president to experience the tragic. This Antonio with his peasant's face dried by the sun has about him the refinement, a gentleness, and a tragic look of Christ in a passion play. His son is a smart, sensitive boy. He is his father's conscience, we are told, and he is ours too. And so is the mother with her sad eyes. She too understands everything. De Sica does not sentimentalize these people. They are not angels. His art is in the clear vision of their predicament and in the many luminous details of their daily lives.

What make both art and memory durable are the details—

the poetry of details. Antonio and Maria riding the bike at dusk from the pawnshop as if they were young lovers. Some little kid playing the accordion and his buddy begging, while Antonio puts up the poster of Rita Hayworth. The pervert who wants to buy Bruno a bell for the bike at the flea market. The jabbering German seminarians hiding from the rain in a doorway with Antonio and Bruno. The soup kitchen where the rich purify the souls of the poor with a sermon before they serve them potatoes and noodles. The father making his son calculate, with a stub of a pencil on a small piece of paper, how much money he would have made on the job he is about to lose.

Each scene in the movie is not only visually interesting but is also wise. Like the pots on the stove in the thief's kitchen over which his mother fusses, these people, one realizes, are even poorer than the victim. And yet none of this appears contrived, staged, to carry a "message." De Sica knows the poor lie and steal but that's no reason not to love them. "That boy wouldn't hurt a fly," someone says about the thief, and we in the audience crack up.

When Antonio decides to steal a bicycle himself, we understand his reasoning: I need a bicycle to feed my family, and here are hundreds of bicycles outside a soccer stadium, where a game has just ended. There's a great shot of the father and son sitting on the curb, the crowd of happy faces streaming by after their team's victory. We know Antonio will get caught, and he does. With the first cry of "Thief," he will be brought down from the stolen bike. "Nice thing you're teaching your son," says someone in the crowd. But what precisely, given our miserable lives, would any parent in postwar Europe teach his children? De Sica avoids any neat summations. At the end of the movie the father and son are walking with tears in their eyes holding each other by the hand. They have their love for each other but not much else. But what a love that is!

Many of us in the audience saw the tragedy as the result of the wife failing to pay the psychic who predicted that her husband will get a job. Antonio suspects it too, and that's why he returns to consult the woman about the stolen bike in her crowded bedroom, where everybody listens to everybody else's troubles. He pays her, but now it's too late. The seer says and repeats,

"Either you find it now, or you never will," and we understand that it's not only the bike she means as she glances at the window, beyond which is Rome and farther beyond, of course, my Belgrade.

8

My own situation was desperate. I couldn't even talk about it with my closest friends. For some reason they were still attending the old school. They had no idea what I was up to. I had to pretend and invent elaborate lies about my activities in school. In fact, I lied all the time. It was a relief when the authorities caught up with me and officially expelled me for truancy.

Still, all in all, what an adventure! I knew every corner, every store window, in that city. I can see clearly each dusty item in a poor shoe repairs window on a street in a quiet, residential neighborhood. I would stop by every time I was in the area and examine that window with the leisure of someone who has nothing to do and nowhere to go.

Once, looking into that window, I saw my mother reflected in the glass hurrying by on the other side of the street. I held my breath and continued to study the shoe trees and the cans of shoe polish, which somehow I knew were empty. They had a foreign brand name. "Kiwi," I said to myself. "Kiwi." I said it again and again standing there.

"You are going to America some day to live with your father," people told me. I never believed it for a moment. It didn't seem possible that I would ever leave this street, this dusty store window where my mother's reflection had just passed. I was afraid to turn around. It was fine just as it was.

In retrospect, it's fortunate I did go to America. Had I stayed, I would have ended up in a reform school. Some of my friends did. I was certainly no better. When I went back to school the following September, one grade behind my classmates, I hated the place. I knew it was just a matter of time before I'd get in trouble again.

In the summer I was usually packed off to my grandfather in the country. This was my mother's father, who had a house and a big orchard in the village where he was born. He lived there alone most of the time taking care of himself as best as he could. By the time I knew him, my grandfather had been in retirement almost thirty years. He was a distinguished-looking and humorless man. His father was a priest, and so were his grandfather and great-grandfather. He himself was an officer who had taken part in the assassination of a Serbian king in 1905.

With other young officers he broke into the royal bedroom and found the king and the queen hiding in the closet or under the bed—I forget which. The king asked for mercy, offered riches, promotions. My grandfather didn't actually participate in their slaying, or so it was said in our family, but who the hell knows! Soon after, he was promoted to captain by the new king.

He had a short and distinguished military career. He was made colonel in World War I after he took his troops into an attack one snowy night somewhere in Macedonia. He said afterward that he was cold in his tent, couldn't sleep, and wanted to warm himself up by leading a charge.

After the war ended, the king pensioned him off in his fortieth year. Didn't want the hothead around. Kept an eye on him too. Local yokels, inducted to be police spies, watched him nap under the huge oak tree in his yard. He wore a straw hat and a white suit and used a cane to keep away the village dogs.

It was torture staying with him. As he was a famous hypochondriac, there were all kinds of dietary prohibitions and obsessions with hygiene. As for conversation, his only topics were his imaginary maladies and the clergy. He hated priests. Later on, when his wife died, he would not permit one at the funeral. It was because of his father, people said, sighing. A first-class son of a bitch. The priests were as bad as most generals. Scum of the earth.

There was a local priest notorious in the area for riding everywhere on his black horse. He'd ride past our house often, slowing down each time to wave to my grandfather. The old man sitting under the oak tree made no acknowledgment of his presence. It embarrassed me. Everywhere I went in the village people gave me a funny look. The kids teased me about my crazy grandfather. I even got into a couple of fights about it. Even though I spent many summers in that place I never made any friends there. I felt superior coming from the city, and local kids felt superior to me because of their knowledge of country ways.

I couldn't wait for the summer to end. There were always important revisions of the pecking order waiting for me in my neighborhood. One had to be reinstated into that tiered world again. There were even new words, slang expressions one had never heard before and which everybody now used all the time. I was afraid to ask what they meant. I'd hear them every day, even use them myself, but it took weeks before I was in the know. In the meantime, I felt like a stranger, as I was to feel so many times in my life.

9

I leave the dentist's chair after what seems an eternity. It's an evening in June. I'm walking the tree-lined streets full of dark, whispering trees in my neighborhood in Belgrade. The streets are poorly lit, but there are a few people about strolling close to each other as if they were lovers. The thought crosses my mind that this is the happiest moment in my life.

What my secretive mother didn't tell me was that there was a good chance we would be leaving Yugoslavia. She had applied for a passport, since the relationship between Yugoslavia and the United States had improved enough for the Communists to permit a few people to leave. The problem was that there was an American quota, a long waiting list for Yugoslavs applying to immigrate to the United States. One just had to wait, but my mother was afraid to wait in Belgrade because the authorities often changed their mind and took the passports back. The moment she got ours, she decided to leave for Paris the very same night. Her brother was living there. We would stay with him, or he would help us find a modest room, while my father, who was already in America, would send us money and support us while we waited for the visa.

I was playing basketball in the neighborhood that afternoon in June 1953 when my mother summoned me and informed me that we were going on vacation immediately. This was very strange. There had been nothing said previously about any vacation on the Dalmatian coast. She was packing feverishly, wanted me to hurry up too, and make no noise. "Don't ask so many questions," she kept saying again and again.

"Why are we taking so many suitcases?" I wanted to know. "Why were our relatives coming to see us with tears in their eyes?

Why was I not permitted to say goodbye to my friends?" I was confused. My mother's gone crazy, I thought. We had plenty of certified lunatics in the family to serve as her model. My great aunt Marina, for instance, or whatever she was to me! She wore old-fashioned black dresses, sang and smiled to herself, and never went out. By the time I was ten I knew there was something out of whack with her.

Our train left at ten that night, but only the following day as we were approaching the Italian border did my mother reveal to me the true destination of our journey. I was stunned. Before I could get over my astonishment, we were in Trieste, that long-yearned-for, almost mythical Trieste where my father had lived after the war. At the train station I ran out and bought some ice cream for all of us. It seemed incredible. All around me now people spoke Italian like in the De Sica movie. The Milan station was even bigger. We ate some sandwiches, and I drank my first Coca-Cola. Little by little, I was beginning to enjoy myself and look forward to what was coming.

It took us almost two days to reach Paris. We were dead tired, of course. My uncle met us at the station. We were taken to a small, seedy hotel, where we took the smallest room that had one double bed and one window. My mother and brother slept on the bed, and I slept on the floor. That's how we lived for one full year. It was a shock. We were poor, I realized. That first evening strolling along the Champs-Elysées, and many times afterward, I became aware that our clothes were ugly. People stared at us. My pants were too short. My jacket was of an absurd, never-seen-before cut. Waiters in cafes approached us cautiously. We had the appearance of customers who do not leave a tip. In stores they eyed us as potential shoplifters. Everybody was astonished when we brought out the money. Even young women at the open market selling apricots and cherries held the bills up to the light. After a couple of weeks in France, I knew I had a new identity. I was a suspicious foreigner from now on.

My mother wasn't going to buy us any new clothes. "You'll get everything new in America," she kept telling us. That took much longer than we anticipated. By the end of summer, it was clear we might remain in Paris for a while. She thought the best thing for my brother and me was to attend school and learn French. I had studied the language in school in Yugoslavia and knew just enough to feel embarrassed every time I opened my mouth. For my brother it was easier. He was only eight years old and didn't care how the words came out.

The school we were enrolled in was for children who were not meant to have a higher education. The French weed out the dummies at an early age and consign them to a permanent inferior status. I felt pretty inferior myself. I couldn't do the schoolwork even on this level. The teachers were not helpful. It was as if they did not really believe that I could not speak French. Perhaps I was just pretending, trying to make a fool of them! They kept giving me zeros. In every subject, on every test and written assignment, I got a zero. At first I was upset and tried harder, but the zeros kept coming, so I gave up.

My classmates generally took no interest in me. The rare few who did were the troublemakers, the class idiots. I made friends with that bunch, which only confirmed my teachers' opinion of me. I was now one of the irremediable. They told me so themselves many times in front of the class, while I counted the flyspecks on the ceiling and debated in my mind the pros and cons of punching them in the mouth.

One of the advantages of being in school, as far as my mother was concerned, was that we got free lunch there. The rest of the time we cooked in my uncle's apartment, or we ate sandwiches in our hotel room. We almost never ate in restaurants. We didn't have much money, and my mother was a type of person who didn't care what she ate. The only experience of French cuisine that I had was at school. I held a high opinion of our cooks that my classmates didn't share. They thought the food was fit for pigs, which meant that I got to eat their portions too. I especially loved the thick vegetable soup that everyone else loathed. I'd eat three or four plates of it. This made it very difficult to stay awake after lunch. Once I fell asleep while drawing a plaster statue of some Greek goddess. "Simic! Simic," I still hear Monsieur Bertrand hollering.

That school year lasted a hundred years, and it was always raining—it was always cold! You don't have to believe me, but that's how it was in Paris. Always gray, always drizzly!

To make things even worse, one day I have an ear infection and am in terrible pain. My mother is taking me to a hospital on the other side of the city because my uncle knows a doctor who will, supposedly, take good care of me. He's going to pierce my eardrum and let the pus out. That's what she tells me on the way to cheer me up. She's an expert on all the details because that's what they did to her when she was a little girl. She even describes the length of the needle to be used. You might conclude my mother has a streak of cruelty in her, but that's not it. She is just dopey.

We are riding in the Metro, which is crowded with people going to work. Nobody looks very happy, but it's perfectly clear to me they're not suffering from earaches. They have a confidence about them. This is their city. The beautiful women have their powdered noses raised high. They can smell a foreigner with a head full of pus on this train.

The hospital is old. It has a high wall and a guarded gate just like a military prison. You can tell immediately a lot of people croaked in there. The walls inside are peeling, and the floors are dirty. The nurses are in foul moods. The patients in the crowded waiting room look resigned to a long wait. Some of them have their eyes closed.

We sit and wait. I'm in great pain. I sit staring at the floor. Then I stare at somebody's shoes as if they were the most interesting thing in the world. Time has no meaning. This must be what eternity is like. A pair of man's black shoes worn by an old woman you stare at forever and ever.

When we finally see the doctor, he's cheerful. A good-looking guy flirting with the nurses even as we come in. No needles for me today, just some penicillin and codeine. Yugoslavs are such wonderful people, he assures us. He's been there to some kind of conference, so he knows. He also likes Marshall Tito. One of the world's great leaders. We agree just to make him happy. Yes, yes, "homme magnifique."

All of a sudden, he's thinking! How come we left glorious Yugoslavia, and so forth? My mother tells him about my father in America, her longing to be reunited with her husband, but we can see he's growing suspicious. Are we some kind of Nazi collaborators, or worse? Who else would leave Yugoslavia, which, as everybody knows, is heaven on earth.

This sort of thing happens often. The leftists are sure we were Fascists and the rightists that we are Commies. Telling our life story makes it even worse, especially the part about my father leaving during the war for Italy when only the Nazis could travel. Even I have to admit it sounds fishy. Our doctor is no longer friendly, and the nurses look as if they were sorry there were no needle.

On the street it's still raining. My ear is still hurting, but I don't mind it so much. And besides, I have an excuse not to go to school for a few days at least.

Our sole entertainment in Paris was walking. We walked even in the rain to get away from our hole in the wall. The moment our dinner was over—which we usually ate early—we'd take off. Every day we'd choose another part of the city. If we had money we'd take the Metro to some distant point and walk back. The idea was to eventually see all of Paris, which we certainly did. Still, there were favorite neighborhoods where we went again and again, like the one around the Opera or the fancy shops on Rue Saint Honore. We each had a favorite shop window. We'd pay them a visit every week the way other people went to the movies. They were mostly clothing stores and car showrooms. One of us would stand there admiring the display, while the other two would grow impatient and start walking away after a while.

I also walked alone. Late at night as my mother and brother were falling asleep, I'd slip out of the room, supposedly to get some fresh air, and go roaming. At that hour I always went to the Champs-Elysées, which was a short distance away and usually hopping. There were, of course, many movie houses and cafes, but there were also nightclubs, the Lido being the most famous one. I'd stand at the entrance, watching people going in and out. Some of them could have been movie stars. They wore dark glasses at night, which impressed me tremendously. I bought a cheap pair, which I wore while watching the beautiful women and their elegant beaus stumble tipsily toward the waiting limousines. I'd hang around as if expecting them to invite me along.

Nobody ever even glanced at me, but that was all right. It was better than lying on that hard hotel floor listening to my mother and brother snore and talk in their sleep.

Once or twice I forgot myself. Suddenly it was very late. The night had turned cold; the great avenue was empty and its cafes and movies were shutting down. I'd hurry home, taking the Avenue Victor Hugo, which was equally deserted and very dark, as it was lined with big trees that obscured the street-lights. I couldn't see a thing, and I was shivering. Then I remembered to remove my glasses. It was much better. A street of massive old buildings, every one of their windows dark. It was a memorable moment. I had a very clear sense of myself existing right then and there—alone, deeply moved.

Some nights I went to the movies with some of the bad boys from school. My mother let me go, figuring it would improve my French. She had no idea what kind of company I was keeping. At first it was to the movies we went. Afterward we only pretended to do that and went instead to Pigalle and Place Blanche and ogled the hookers. We started dressing up too. I wore a tie, kept my hair slicked down, and smoked cigarettes in the French manner, with the butt hanging from the corner of my mouth. Nobody took us seriously. We had no money for the girls. We were hoping for charity, love at first sight. The problem was we had to be home by a certain hour. Whatever opportunities presented themselves long past midnight, we were never to find out.

These French boys I hung around with were very nice. They came from poor families. Now that they were doing badly in school, they knew their lives would be hard. They had absolutely no illusions about that. In the meantime, they had the street smarts, the humor and appetite for adventure, that reminded me of the friends I had left behind in Belgrade. Even with my limited French, we understood one another perfectly. They'd kid me about this or that, but it was all good-natured. Of course, they knew everything about what goes on in Paris.

One afternoon I went to a nudie show with a friend. I remember that we thought about it for a long time before we actually got the courage to do it. We were afraid they would turn us away, laugh us off. This was one of the cheapest joints. Nobody asked any questions. We found ourselves in an almost empty theater. We sat right in front after first trying the back. There was a show with a male singer and a comedian. The women were ancient, or so it seemed to us. Huge thighs and busts and plenty of rolls of fat in between. From where we sat we could see the stretch marks and scars on their bodies. They wore rhinestone-studded pasties and G-strings. The whole thing was shabby, badly done. I remember blushing. We didn't stay for the whole show.

10

It's still 1953. I'm a fifteen-year-old immigrant living in Paris. I hate school. The teachers can't bear the sight of me and are most likely delighted when I stay away. I'm flunking every subject except for art, where I have a passing grade. I don't speak or write French very well, but the heartless bastards are not buying my excuse, so I skip classes every time I figure I can get away with it. I roam the streets until it's time to return home. Home is a hotel room where my mother sits waiting for me with my younger brother, who attends a different school. We have only one bed. They have it to themselves, while I sleep on the floor usually fully dressed because of the dampness. One needs a mattress, or so I discovered, to toss and turn sleepless and philosophize. On the hard floor the minute I stir awake, I sit up rubbing my aching muscles and bones and think about school. Our math teacher, Monsieur Bertrand, often makes me stand in the corner for the slightest transgressions, as if I were a little kid. This is okay with me. I don't mind spending the entire day with my face to the wall. I can take my time reviewing some movie I've liked recently. Once a schoolmate had to tap me on a shoulder to bring me back from Los Angeles, since I had not heard the teacher order me back to my seat. Forty-five years later I still dream about that corner. Everyone has gone home and left me. Night has fallen, and I'm cooling my heels. When I peek over my shoulder, the six windows of the classroom are black and wet with rain. I do not know whether to leave or keep waiting for the teacher to return and give me permission. It's a dream in which absolutely nothing happens and from which I still awaken sad and full of fear.

It would make sense to play hooky on warm, sunny days, but that's not what happens. The more miserable the weather, the more I want to cut and run. Monday mornings are the worst. To economize, I don't ride the Metro. I hug the buildings as I make my way in the rain toward the Grand Boulevards, where there are arcades, department stores, lobbies of movie houses, and other such spots where I can find shelter and pass the day. One time I even hid in a church. The lone old woman crossing herself gave me a worried look. She was afraid to kneel down and pray with her back turned to me. In a photo I have from this period, I'm wearing a baggy dark overcoat with a raised collar and a pair of lighter pants so wrinkled and frayed at the cuffs, I'm surprised my mother let me go out looking like that. I have no hat and positively need a haircut, or at least a comb. From the stares I've gotten from salespeople, I know better than to set foot into finer stores. In spite of all that, my expression in the photograph is unmistakably cheerful. My feet and coat may be soaked, but I'm on my way to meet Gene Tierney.

With the little moolah I usually had, I could not afford the first-run movie palaces. I frequented and knew well all the small, seedy movie houses in the city. My favorite haunts were the several cinemas on Avenue des Ternes, a hole-in-the-wall on Avenue des Grand Armée where they showed only westerns, the theaters off Boulevard Saint Michel in the Latin Quarter where Sorbonne students went to neck, and Cinema Mac Mahon on the avenue of the same name where I saw *Singing in the Rain* a dozen times.

My rule was, if it was an American movie, I'd most likely go in. My mother would drag us to French movies, but by myself I only recollect seeing the ones forbidden to minors where someone like Martin Carol, so I heard in school, bared her boobs. On rainy mornings most cashiers didn't care how old I was. By today's standards it was all pretty chaste. A quick peep is all one could hope for. Yes, there was more ass and tits in French flicks, but juvenile delinquents tend to be Romantics at heart. Plus, I had become deeply enamored of American films noir.

I had no idea they were called that, of course. I had seen *Asphalt Jungle* and *Key Largo* in Belgrade, liked them tremendously, and sought their match. Every movie house in those days displayed stills of the film being shown, so one could get an idea. One peek, and I knew. If there were a tough guy in a raincoat pointing a revolver or some blonde puffing away while showing a lot of leg perched on a bar stool, I'd dash in, often in the middle of the film. I'd find myself right off on an empty street at night. A few silver clouds are visible above the dark skyscrapers, and a sinister-looking parked car waits for me up ahead. Since I had no idea of the plot, such scenes stood out. I studied every face, every shadowy interior, as if it were a tarot card and I an apprentice fortune-teller. I was intimate with Veronica Lake, Lauren Bacall, Ida Lupino, and even Gloria Graham, but I had never before laid eyes on Tierney until *Laura*.

We met in an old, cavernous theater on Avenue des Ternes. A dozen customers sitting far apart. The superfluous, familiar usherette who took me to my seat in the dark house and pocketed the tip. If I, or anyone else, didn't have the right amount, she was sure to return, point the flashlight at your face, and chew you out for being a cheapskate even in front of the full house. I usually counted the tip over and over again before handing it to her, and even then I sat in terror for the first fifteen minutes of the movie.

Laura is a murder mystery that begins with the beautiful heroine already dead. An oil painting of the victim that hangs in her elegant apartment obsesses the detective investigating the case. He gradually falls in love with the dead woman, and so did I watching the movie. Laura, to everybody's surprise, reappears alive and is no less mysterious than she was during her disappearance. The other characters and the various turns of the plot meant much less to me. It's Tierney, with her cool, dark-haired, slinky beauty, who got to me that day. With her air of refinement and her upper-class accent, she came across as the soul of kindness and understanding. And yet, as much as I studied her, she always remained for me a masque, a tantalizing enigma. "Friends came to her at odd hours of the day and night," one of the characters says in the film. In odd moments she could have been an expensive call girl or a Chinese opium addict. I remember creeping up all the way to the front row to scrutinize her up close.

I stayed for the next show and the next. I was in big trouble, and still I was in no rush to leave my seat. It occurred to me, I could slip behind one of the heavy curtains, stay hidden throughout the night, and resume watching her tomorrow at noon. I was sorely tempted. It was hard to exit so erotically charged into the dark, rainy afternoon, guilty about missing school, knowing my mother is going crazy with worry. "Death is the mother of beauty," the poet says. You bet! I was as scared to death of my inner turmoil as I was of meeting my mother.

Several days passed before I could see the movie again. Then the program changed. There were no more Tierney films shown anywhere in Paris. Every day I checked the newspapers and weekly entertainment magazines to make sure but had no luck. Since they did not list all the actors appearing in a movie, it was prudent to crisscross Paris and examine in person the posters of the films shown that week.

In the meantime, like the film's title song, I couldn't get her out of my head. So what if the girls my age took no notice of me? I was strolling the streets arm in arm with my secret companion. Of course, she had no time for small talk. She let me soliloquize. I poured my heart out to her—but in what language? My English was poor, my French not much better—so it must have been a pidgin of the two with a few words of Serbo-Croatian thrown in. In any case, I also became fussy with my appearance. I greased my hair, and I started wearing a bright red tie, which I bought off some Arabs on Rue de Temple. My mother kept irritating me by maintaining that only Communists wear red ties. All I needed, she said, is *L'Humanité*, the party newspaper, sticking out of my pocket.

I spent hours in front of the mirror. Sometimes Laura joined me there. I saw myself as a very young Richard Basehart, with that sensitive, intelligent mug of his. Then I'd catch my brother behind me trying to imitate my expression, and we would both burst out laughing, or my mother would begin to nag me about homework. Sitting around the hotel room with him on the floor playing with his cars and her boiling another pot of noodles cannot have been much fun for Miss Tierney.

My complicated imaginary life reminds me now of Buster Keaton's in *Sherlock Jr.*, where he plays a movie projectionist who dreams himself into a film shown on the screen. The audience watches him walk straight into the screen and become part of the action. Once there, he's at the mercy of the way the scenes are being cut. He enters a living room, the living room vaporizes, and he finds himself at the front door. He knocks, but just then there's another cut and the steps and the yard are gone. He tries to sit down but finds himself amidst the rushing traffic with cars just barely missing him. Next he is on a hilltop, then in a forest between two lions. When they, too, vanish, he's in a desert about to be run down by a train. Next, he's on a rock in the sea. He dives into the waves but ends up in a snowbank. He extricates himself and is back in the front yard where it all started. Inside the house a man and a woman are still smooching.

That's how it was with Tierney and me. We were playing hide-and-seek between dream and reality. One minute I was having lunch with her at the Algonquin, the next we were standing outside a jazz club on Rue Saint André listening to Don Byas play "Laura" through the half-open door. Even if I had had the money, they would not have let me in, especially talking to myself like that. "Dames are always pulling a switch on you," Dana Andrews, who plays the detective assigned to the case, confided to me. I could readily agree with that.

To complicate matters even further, I finally saw another Tierney movie. It was called *Leave Her to Heaven*, and it was dubbed. She was babbling in French. I forgot to mention earlier that I had an aversion to dubbed films, always went exclusively to what was known as v.o. (original version), but, in my rush to see my dreamboat, I failed to notice the flaw.

In this film mademoiselle is a murderess and a suicide. We meet her first in a club car of a train. She has dozed off, and the book she was reading has slid off her knees, so Cornell Wilde runs over to pick it up. She comes to, snazzy as ever, thanks him in that calm, whispery voice of hers, and he's hooked. The film is in color, so I learn that her eyes are blue. She has the habit of drawing close to the person she's talking to as if she were nearsighted or a bit hard of hearing. I find this very disconcerting.

The chump who retrieved the book is a writer, actually the author of the book she was reading. Tierney plays a woman who, after they are married, is jealous of everyone and everything, including her husband spending hours at the typewriter away from her. Even his crippled, teenage brother is a rival, so one day she takes him out in a rowboat on a lake, urges him to swim a good distance, and, when he begins to flail and call for her help, she stops rowing, calmly reaches over, puts on her sunglasses, and watches him drown.

Even viler is a beach scene following the death of her unborn son, which she contrives by intentionally falling down a flight of stairs. Stunning in a tight red bathing suit, she frolics in the surf, runs up to towel herself, smiling and making me quake in my seat. This woman is a handful, I realized. No more sunset walks by the Seine for us or cow-eyed holding of hands in Luxembourg Park. It was no joke having a felon even for an imaginary friend. What a good time she was having being bad. How confusing it all was. My head was telling me one thing, while my crotch muttered something else. I walked out of the theater dazed, only to be blinded further by the sunlight. I remember I had to shelter my eyes to make my way slowly toward the Metro on Place Saint Michel. It was the first truly warm spring day. Everywhere, so I noted squinting, there were young women fleeting about lightly dressed, one or two of whom I even followed a little way until they vanished in the afternoon crowd.

11

The most important thing we did in Paris was study English. My mother found out that there were free night classes, twice a week, given by the World Church Service. All three of us went. Previously, I don't believe I knew ten words of English. My mother knew some, but not much. In any case, here we were in a class with a bunch of refugees from all over Eastern Europe and a very friendly American minister as a teacher. I worked hard for once. I liked the language immediately.

We began buying the *Saturday Evening Post* and *Look* magazine to practice reading. I understood little of what I read, but the pictures and advertisements were very interesting. The American colors were so bright. One didn't see such yellows, reds, and oranges in Europe. The pictures of children terrified me; they looked so clean, so happy. The girls often had freckles. They smiled a lot. Everybody smiled. The old people with perfect teeth, the movie stars, the politicians, too, all had their mouths stretched from ear to ear. In France nobody smiled like that. Certainly not the barbers. I remember a Norman Rockwell–like cover of a little redhead kid in a barber's chair with a smiling barber bending over him with scissors. The barbers in Paris gave me dirty looks when I walked in to have one of my rare haircuts.

When we went to the American Embassy for the obligatory physical examination given to every prospective immigrant, I expected the doctor to be grinning. He looked glum while he listened to my chest. I must be very sick, I told myself. None of the nurses smiled either. It was clear; I'd be rejected. My brother and mother will go to America, and I'll stay here in France wasting away from some incurable disease in a crowded and filthy state hospital.

Weeks passed before we got the results of the examination. In the meantime, we worried and turned the pages of American magazines, studying the cars, the baked hams out of a can, the rich, many-layered desserts. The summer was approaching. We walked all the time. One evening, just after dusk, on the fashionable Avenue Victor Hugo, we saw Prince Paul, the brother of the assassinated Yugoslav King who himself was deposed in 1941 in an act that got Yugoslavia into the war. My mother went up to him to say we were Yugoslavs. I remember an impeccably dressed, elderly man bowing stiffly to my mother and asking me my name. I could tell he didn't care one way or another what it was.

In those days, both in Paris and United States, we ran into famous politicians, people who were responsible, if anyone was solely responsible, for Yugoslavia's troubles. Here, sitting in somebody's kitchen slicing salami, would be a face you remembered from an old newspaper, signing some treaty with Hitler or Mussolini. It was hard to believe they were the same people. They looked pretty ordinary and talked nonsense just like everybody else. They expected to return next week and no later than the week after. Their villas and bank accounts would be restored. Great crowds would welcome them, shouting, "You were right! You were always right!" They didn't like one bit what my mother and I had to say about Yugoslavia. They insisted that nothing had changed since they left. They felt sorry for us falling so obviously for Commie propaganda.

In early June of 1954 we received our American visas. It took several more weeks to book our passage. The World Church Service paid our way and in style. We were to sail on the *Queen Mary* on August 5. What excitement! "You'll be starting a whole new life," everybody said. Even our grocer was sure it was going to be wonderful.

Our remaining days in Paris dragged on. My mother took us to museums daily so we'd remember the great art treasures of France. We also started eating modest meals in modest neighborhood restaurants. At night we went to the movies, watching the American films from the first rows, looking for clues to our future.

In school I had flunked everything except drawing and music, so I avoided my friends. I was ashamed of myself. After the terror of waiting for the results of my physical, I felt somewhat more optimistic but not entirely. Who could be sure I was not going to be a complete failure in America?

The *Queen Mary* was all lit up the night we boarded it. It was huge and a veritable labyrinth on the inside. We were traveling in the cheapest class, but the accommodations seemed luxurious to us. It took a couple of days to discover that we were not supposed to leave our class. There was a door with a sign that spelled it out. I snuck through it once, walked through the magnificent Cabin Class, and made my way to the First Class. There were shops and restaurants there as elegant as anything they have in Paris. I saw ladies in evening gowns cut so low their breasts were about to fall out, men in dark suits smoking cigars, little children who wore neckties and looked snotty. I remember a bejeweled old woman in a wheelchair pushed by a very beautiful nurse in white. It didn't take long before a steward spotted me ogling and directed me politely back to the Tourist Class.

We had no complaints about our class. Far from it. Our cabins were small and windowless but otherwise comfortable. The food was excellent, and there was a new film shown every day. Everybody was friendly and in a good mood, especially at the beginning of the trip.

A day or two after we left Le Havre there was a storm. It started during the night. The ship heaved and creaked as if starting to come apart. It was impossible to sleep, and many got seasick. In the morning only a few showed up for breakfast. By the afternoon, with the storm still raging, the movie theater was empty. They showed the movie anyway. The boat rocked, the waves pounded its sides, but the people on the screen went on talking with perfect composure.

My mother was back in the cabin throwing up, but my brother and I refused to stay in bed. We liked the food so much, we didn't allow ourselves to get sick. We roamed our section of the ship. It was difficult to walk, of course. We had to hold onto the walls and railings. It never occurred to us to be scared. We sat in the empty lounge for hours watching the waves crest and slide under the ship. There was a lot of water out there. It was absolutely amazing. We couldn't get over it.

The next day the storm subsided. The sky was cloudless. The chart outside the purser's office indicated the progress of our voyage. We were more than halfway across. The next day we were even closer. We kept asking the crew when we would be able to see the land.

The sighting occurred at night. By the time we rose in the morning the land was clearly visible. We were speeding into the New York harbor. After breakfast everyone was on deck. We began to make out details on the land. There was a road on which a car was traveling. Everybody kept pointing to it! Next, there were some neat white houses. One even had laundry hung out to dry in its backyard. Then a fishing boat came by. There were a couple of black men on deck, waving. Pretty soon there were small boats everywhere. We could see the Statue of Liberty. I think a cheer went up.

What stunned me, left me speechless with excitement, was the first sight of Manhattan with its skyscrapers. It was just like in the movies, except this was the real thing. The enormous city before us with its docks, its big ships, its traffic on the outer highways, its billboards and crowds. My father was out there somewhere waiting for us. We tried to spot him. We didn't realize we would have to go back down and spend hours clearing immigration. With our past experiences of border crossing, we were a bit nervous. You never knew. What if they pulled a surprise on us and sent us back to Yugoslavia?

My father waited past the customs. A tall man. We recognized him from the pictures. We waved. He waved back. He was wearing a white suit under which we could see a blue shirt and suspenders. Very American, we thought. He smoked a long thin cigar and smiled in a friendly way.

Then the confusion of embraces and kisses, the emotion of his seeing my brother for the first time, the search for a porter, the wait for a taxi, and everybody talking at the same time. It was all incredible and wonderful! The trash on the streets, the way people were dressed, the tall buildings, the dirt, the heat, the yellow cabs, the billboards and signs. It was nothing like Europe. It was terrifically ugly and beautiful at the same time! I liked America immediately.

In the hotel room another surprise awaited us. There was a

television set. While my mother and father talked, my brother and I sat on the floor and watched a Dodgers-Giants game. I remember who was playing because my brother fell in love with baseball that afternoon, and with the Dodgers in particular, and insisted on being outfitted immediately with a baseball cap and glove.

That evening, after a stroll around Times Square and Broadway, we went to a restaurant where we dined on hamburgers, french fries, and milk shakes, followed by banana splits. I don't know what my mother thought of the meal, but we loved it. American food is kid's food, and no kid in the world can resist it. "Remember this day," my father kept saying. Indeed, it was August 10, 1954. Tomorrow he was going to buy us American clothes and shoes and all sorts of other things.

Who could possibly sleep? My mother and brother did. My father and I watched TV and talked. It was still early. "Let's go for a walk," he said. The hotel was only a couple of blocks away from Times Square. We found ourselves there again, watching the crowd. I felt comfortable with my father right away. He never treated anyone younger differently. He talked to everybody the same way. He would address a five-year-old selling lemonade on the street as if he were the head of a major corporation.

We ended up in a jazz club that night. It was called the Metropole, on Broadway and Forty-eighth Street. A long narrow room with a bar on one side and small booths on the other. The bandstand was just above the bar. There were six black musicians blasting away.

We took a booth, and my father ordered some whiskey for himself and ginger ale for me. This must have been some day for him too. I was all absorbed in the music. This was definitely better than any radio. It was heaven.

We stayed a long time. My father even gave me a few sips of his whiskey. Between sets we talked. I told him about my life, and he told me about his. This was just the beginning. We spent many nights together like that. My father loved the nightlife. He was happiest in bars and restaurants. In the company of friends and with something good to eat and drink, he'd glow. It was pure joy to be around him then. He was full of life and interesting talk. I didn't want to go to bed, but we finally had to.

"This is wonderful," he said. He always wanted to come to America and had a chance to do so when, in 1926, he won some kind of scholarship to Columbia University, but then he didn't, to his everlasting regret and for reasons that were entirely trivial. "Even in prison in Italy," he told me, "I sat in solitary confinement dreaming of New York."

One morning the Germans took him out into the courtyard at daybreak, and he figured they were going to shoot him. There was a squad of armed soldiers and an officer with them, but then a photographer with a tripod came and took several pictures of my father standing against the wall. He had no idea what for.

"I want to see New York before I die," he told the Germans as they were leading him back to his cell.

My father was still employed by the same telephone company he used to work for back in Yugoslavia. Their headquarters were in Chicago, but he spent all his time on the road. Whenever one of their client companies needed more telephone lines, my father was sent to examine the facilities, draw up the blueprints, and stay there until the job was completed. As it was, he spent the years 1950–54 moving from one small town to another, spending in each place anywhere from a couple of months to a year. He had no home. At the time we arrived, he was working in Middletown, New York. After his vacation was over, and having found an apartment for us in Queens, he went back to Middletown. I went with him.

The idea was, I would study English on my own and not enroll in school till the second semester. We would spend the week in Middletown and come to New York on weekends. That's what we did. I stayed in the rooming house, while my father worked. In the evenings we ate out then either went to the movies or came back to our room to talk and drink wine.

My father, as was his custom, had a lot of books, two trunks full. At that time his ambition was to write a critical history of Marxism, so most of the books were on that subject. He read late into the night and took voluminous notes. He made occasional comments about the project as he told me about his life. There was his life, and there was Marxism and fascism and everything else. He was trying to make sense of it all.

His stories were tremendously entertaining. He was also interested in my own. We had a lot of catching up to do. What made it exciting for me was that for the first time in my life I could be absolutely frank. I told him everything, and he did the same to me. We were both, in our own way, very lonely people. The ten years that we didn't see each other made it difficult to reestablish our relationship on a father-son basis. It was much easier to be friends, to talk like friends. When people overheard us they were shocked. "The way that boy speaks to his father!"

During this time he was teaching me English. The first book I read in English was Whittaker Chambers's *Witness*. I don't remember a thing about it today, but at that time it gave me the confidence necessary to attempt to read others. When in New York, my father would spend Saturday mornings going from bookstore to bookstore. He bought books, and it was understood I could pick some for myself. I did that often, picking out something much too difficult for me. I read Hemingway and Twain and God-knows-what-else! It was a slow process, since I had to look up a lot of words in the dictionary, and there were long passages that I simply didn't understand. Still, I had so much time to myself while he was at work.

My return to school terrified me. It had been a long time since I was properly a student. I had no confidence in my ability. I also had no idea what grade I'd be in. I would see young people my age going to school, and I would shudder. The way I spoke English anybody could tell immediately I was a foreigner.

The closer Christmas came and the beginning of the second semester, the more miserable I became. My father was still a lot of fun, but the mood at home was tense. It was clear my parents were not getting along. The ten years of separation, plus their completely different personalities, made them strangers. Whatever one liked, the other did not. My mother, for example, had no interest in things American. She had already found some Yugoslavs, was seeing them, and, aside from wanting to improve her English so that she could get a job, she had no curiosity about this country. Since my brother and I sided with my father, there were constant conflicts. She grew jealous. "You don't love me anymore," she'd blurt out. "We have more fun with him," we'd make the mistake of saying.

Still, for a while appearances were preserved. We sat around the dinner table making plans for the future. My brother and I would go to college and that sort of thing. I had my doubts, but I said nothing.

The high school I was supposed to attend was in Elmhurst, Queens. My parents had gone there to make inquiries. I was invited to come shortly after the New Year, before the classes resumed, and take some tests so I could be placed in the proper grade.

I didn't sleep the night before the appointment. My father was back in Middletown. It was a windy and bitterly cold morning, and the walk from our place to the school was very long. I was numb with cold and terror when I arrived.

As usually happens in life, things turned out quite differently from what I had anticipated. Luckily, there was no question of writing to Belgrade or Paris for a transcript. The European education system is very different, and it would be very difficult to interpret such a document whenever it eventually arrived. So they made it simple. They gave me an IQ test, and, as for the rest, they just asked me to write down the subjects I had studied in Europe.

That was easy enough. I wrote down things like algebra, physics, French, Russian, world history, biology. They asked me a couple of questions in each area and in the process found out that in Paris we had read Homer and Virgil. That did it. I was made a second-semester junior on the spot. The whole process did not take more than a couple of hours.

I was greatly relieved. I still had some apprehension about actually doing the schoolwork, but this was a miraculous beginning. My love for America was infinite. No more Monsieur Bertrand and his crummy jokes at my expense. Even the Yugoslav teachers had given me hard times after I stayed back. School was not for dummies like me, they reminded me daily. Years later, I heard they were incredulous when told that I had gone to college. "That little bum! Don't Americans have any sense?"

The school itself was amazing. Newton High School may have been the model for the movie *Blackboard Jungle*. I had met all kinds of juvenile delinquents in my life, but never so many. This was like reform school. The teachers had their hands full maintaining discipline. If you kept your mouth shut, as I did, you passed all your subjects.

I remember a large class in something called "Hygiene." I sat in the last row playing chess with a black kid. Up front the teacher was arguing about something with a couple of punks in leather jackets. That's the way it was every day, half of the class harassing the teacher while the other half daydreamed. I never did any work. Nobody called on me. I don't think I even had a clue what I was supposed to do, but I kept my mouth shut. I received a B for my silence at the end of the semester.

The other classes were more or less the same. In English the old lady who was our teacher kept trying to read aloud one of Edgar Allan Poe's tales. The class, against her objections, provided the sound effects. There were the sinister creaking doors and coffin lids, clocks ticking at midnight, and the wind blowing through the ruined tower. She pleaded with us to stop. When we were reading Julius Caesar, it was the same. More sound effects and muffled laughter. I came to see her once after class to ask for an extension on my term paper, blaming my delay on the ignorance of the English language. "Don't worry," the poor woman told me. "I know you're a good boy." I certainly was. I behaved in class and did my homework. The girls interested me, but I was too shy to speak to them in my heavily accented English. As for the boys, many of them were trouble bound, and I'd had enough of that for a while. Also, I had no time to hang around. I was working after school and all day Saturdays.

It was a terrific job as far as I was concerned. I worked for a small company that supplied special screws for airplanes. I helped the stock clerk. I counted screws. The screws were very expensive, so you had to be super-careful counting them. I was. It wasn't difficult, and I got paid. I bought a cheap phonograph and my first jazz records. On Sundays I went to Manhattan and the movies. I was beginning to feel very comfortable in America.

The big event that spring was buying a television set. It was a huge twenty-one-inch model that my father and I had a hell of a time lugging from the store. Once we turned it on, it stayed on. We watched television all the time. It was good for our English, everybody said. It certainly was. I stopped reading books and just watched TV. Everything interesting from breakfast shows to late, late movies. I think that it was while watching television that my brother and I started speaking English to each other. We heard certain expressions on TV and wanted to use them immediately.

I am surprised how quickly we felt at home in the United States. My father's attitude had a lot to do with it. He thought America was the most exciting place on earth and wanted us to share his excitement. He had no desire to go back to Yugoslavia. He wanted us to be real Americans. My mother, on the other hand, had always retained the conviction that Europeans were superior. She missed Europe. I did not. I was a flop there. Here I had managed to finish a grade. I had a job, and summer was coming.

Then we had another surprise. My father's request for a transfer to the company's headquarters, which he didn't expect to be approved, suddenly came through. We were moving to Chicago. From now on we would live together, see him all the time, and have a normal life.

I wasn't entirely happy about being uprooted again, nor was my mother. She worried about leaving New York, where there were more opportunities to find work in the music business. She was trying to resume her career as a voice teacher but had no luck. Still, she also desired some kind of regular family life. There really was not much choice. It was decided that my father and I would go first, find an apartment, and then my mother and brother would follow.

12

It was late in June 1955 when we traveled to Chicago on the train called the Twentieth Century. We were going in style, sleeping in the Pullman berths and taking our meals in the fancy dining car. In Chicago we took a room at the elegant Hotel Drake on Michigan Avenue. The lake was right outside our window. There was a beach we could go to and many fine restaurants and nightclubs in the area. We spent the first two weeks enjoying life and not making the slightest effort to look for a place. When my mother called, we told her it was difficult, the city was so big, and so on.

Again my father and I talked and talked. I was beginning to have a much clearer picture of our family background from these late-hour conversations.

My great-grandfather Philip, for example, was a blacksmith in a small village in Serbia. My great-grandmother had died in childbirth, and he himself took care of his son and daughter. It seems he didn't have any relatives in the area. Earlier his own father, or his grandfather, had migrated to Serbia from Montenegro. My father didn't know for sure.

I liked the stories about this great-grandfather of mine, one of them especially! How he had not been paying taxes for some time and how one day the cops came in force to arrest him. He pleaded with them not to take him away and make his children orphans. He even had a suggestion. What if they were to give him a part-time job at the police station, make him a deputy or something, so he could earn some extra money and pay his taxes?

Well, the cops, being local fellows and knowing Philip, took pity on him. At the police station the arrangements were made. He was issued a rifle and was even given a small advance on his pay for other purchases related to his new duties. There were tears of gratitude on his part, everyone was moved, and after many handshakes Philip left. He made his way straight to the tavern, where he stayed for three days raising hell. When he was thoroughly out of his mind, he made the waiters carry four tables outside at gunpoint. Then he ordered that the tables should be stacked one on top of the other, with a chair and a bottle of booze at the very top. There he climbed, drunk as he was. A crowd had gathered by then. There were Gypsies, too, fiddling and banging on their tambourines. When he started shooting his rifle and shouting that no Simic was ever going to be a stupid cop, the police showed up. They beat the daylights out of him and threw him in jail.

Philip's son, my grandfather Zika, went to Vienna and Prague while still a very young man to learn the tool-and-die trade. Upon his return just before World War I, and over the years, he became the best craftsman in that trade in Belgrade. Following the war, his skills were in such demand that he even became wealthy for a while. Temperamentally, though, he was just like his father. He couldn't keep his money. He hated all middle-class values and institutions. Politicians, priests, and schoolteachers were on his list of contemptible beings. He had absolutely nothing in common with my other grandfather, but they were in agreement. "I only love waiters," I heard him say once.

Nevertheless, he married a schoolteacher's sister. Radojka, my father's mother, bore Zika four children and died from consumption when my father was twelve. As he was the oldest, he took care of the younger ones. Even in the last days of his life, while he lay dying in the hospital in Dover, New Hampshire, my father often spoke of his mother. She sang beautifully and played "every instrument," as he put it. He still remembered the songs she taught him and would try to sing them with tears in his eyes:

> Three meadows and no shade anywhere to be found,
> Three meadows, just an old bare tree . . .

I forget the words exactly, but he never did. He never got over her death. His sorrow for her and her short, unhappy life was greater for him seventy years later than the thought of his own imminent extinction, which he took with a kind of detached amusement.

The relationship to his father was more complex. He told me many times that he didn't want to be the bastard his father had been to him. But then he'd tell me some story about the two of them going drinking together and listening to the Gypsies, and there'd be a lot of affection for his father. All Zika's children—and there were two more from another marriage—had that love-hate relationship with their father.

Be that as it may, here in Chicago my father and I were continuing to live it up. Every night we told ourselves that tomorrow we'd start looking for a place but never did—not, in any case, till my mother informed us that she was coming in a week to help us look. In the meantime, my father was running out of money. He was supposed to resume working soon, but the first paycheck would not be coming for a while, and his savings were gone. One morning he visited a loan company, where he finagled a huge loan. We still had a few days left before my mother's arrival, and we spent them partying. The way my father tipped waiters and bought books and clothes for us made it look as if we would soon be broke again. He'd give a waiter ten dollars the moment he came to our tables with the menus and ask him to take the damn things away and bring us instead a good bottle of wine and not to bother us until we called him again.

That recklessness of his both attracted and drove me crazy. Years later in New York we once spent our monthly rent on a meal in a French restaurant. It was an expensive and fashionable place. We were ushered without much ceremony to a tiny table in the back, where we polished off our appetizers, main course, and a couple of bottles of wine rather quickly and unconsciously, absorbed as we were in some sort of intellectual argument. When the snotty waiter presented us with the bill, we both realized at the very same moment that (1) the service had been lousy; (2) we'd talked too much and hadn't really savored what we were eating and drinking; (3) we were in no rush to go anywhere. Without exchanging a word, we knew what the next step would be. My father informed the waiter that in place of dessert we'd like to have the whole meal repeated, starting with the appetizers and the white wine. "The whole thing once again," I told him, too, just to make sure he understood. The waiter went away and came back, flustered, to ask us to repeat, please, what we'd said. So we did and then resumed our talk. In time they brought the food, which we ate with an even greater appetite. By then the place was emptying. The waiters stood across the room watching us apprehensively. The boss and the cook finally came over with a bottle of fine cognac. "Do you always dine like this?" they wanted to know. "Only when we are hungry," my father assured them.

Three days after my mother arrived in Chicago we found an apartment in Oak Park, a suburb west of the city. My mother got in touch with some Serbians she knew, and they told her that Oak Park was a nice place to live. We took the El one morning, bought the local papers, and by the afternoon had our place. It was on the top floor of a three-story tenement-like building and had two bedrooms, a living room, and a fairly large kitchen. The neighborhood, with its tree-lined streets and one-family homes, was a good one, but the apartment was crummy. In their impatience to find a place, my parents didn't realize there were railroad tracks just outside our back windows. All the trains leaving Union Station for points west roared by, rattling our pots and pans and just about everything else. We were so close to the trains we could see people in the dining car being served by black waiters. We could almost make out what they had on their plates. It didn't occur to my parents to move. I guess they were sick and tired of moving. We just stayed.

I was enrolled in Oak Park's high school. That's the one Ernest Hemingway attended. The teachers reminded us of that every day. My mother found a job in Marshall Field's department store as a seamstress. My brother was in third grade. He was doing great, playing baseball and speaking English better than I did. Life could have been normal, except that my parents were snapping at each other or didn't speak to each other for days. I had the unenviable task of passing messages between them. As far as I was concerned, they were both right and both wrong. I loved them equally but hated having them under the same roof.

My new school was no joke. One had to study, do homework

every night, and be prepared to answer intelligently in class. My classmates were mostly children of professional people and had the confidence and ability of well-brought-up young people. They were very nice to me. I think I was the only foreigner in the school, and so I was a curiosity. Soon enough I began leading the life of a typical small-town teenager. I went to football games and hung around the drug store and hamburger joints frequented by my classmates.

I had some interesting teachers, too. My English teacher, a man by the name of Dolmetsh, took time with me. He realized I was a voracious reader, so he supplied me with books. He gave me Joyce's *Portrait of the Artist as a Young Man* and a number of other contemporary classics to read. A French teacher gave me contemporary French poets. In addition to the books I got in school, I discovered the public library. I couldn't believe that one had the right to take all those wonderful books and records home. I went almost every day and got a new load.

I was also beginning to be interested in painting. I drew, did watercolors, and even some oil paintings that year. This was an important activity. I discovered modern art and its aesthetic. I never had any illusion that I had much talent, and I stopped painting when I was twenty-six years old, but some of the things I did show knowledge of abstract expressionism and are not the worst things ever painted in that idiom.

In school, of course, I gravitated toward students who were interested in the arts. One day two of my friends confessed that they wrote poetry. I asked them to show it to me. I wasn't impressed with what I saw. I went home and wrote some poems myself in order to demonstrate to them how it's supposed to be done. At first the act of writing and the initial impression were exhilarating. Then, to my astonishment, I realized my poems were as stupid as theirs were. I couldn't figure it out. It made me pay attention to poetry in a different way. I went through a couple of anthologies trying to divine the secret. I tried writing again, but it was still no good. To be sure, it all began with my wanting to impress my friends, but then, in the process of writing, I discovered a part of myself, an imagination and a need to articulate certain things, that I could not afterward forget.

13

We all came to America expecting to play a part in a Hollywood movie. Most of the American films were made in southern California, so if you were in Europe, watching those palm trees swaying in the wind with someone like Rita Hayworth gliding underneath them in a white convertible, you got all kinds of wonderfully wrong ideas about the place. Do people really live like that, I wondered? What will they say about my bad teeth and my funny accent? America was a fearful paradise.

It was reassuring to find that in Chicago there were poor people. Trash-strewn streets with laundry hanging from fire escapes. Old men swaying on the corner drinking out of brown paper bags. Kids pummeling each other in a schoolyard. Plenty of beggars. An old woman with a street organ and a monkey. She turned the crank with both hands, while the monkey went around with a tin cup. He wore a tattered coat with brass buttons and looked young and full of mischief. This all I understood. I immediately felt at home.

Chicago in the 1950s was still a town of factories. Its ugliness and squalor brought to mind Dostoyevsky's descriptions of Moscow and St. Petersburg slums. The people waiting for a North Avenue bus looked as if they had just arrived from Ellis Island. Still, there was plenty of work. An immigrant would come to Chicago, get a job in a factory, and keep it for the rest of his life. He would speak some English, some Polish, some Hungarian, and some Italian because these are the languages of the people he worked with. Once upon a time he knew what he was, the culture he belonged to. Now he was no longer sure.

He worked all the time. The immigrants often had the gray, weary look of people working long hours and weekends but they had no complaints about that. The neighborhoods smelled of steaks and fried chicken, where in the old country all you could smell was cabbage. A big temptation for an immigrant with literary pretensions is to leave all that behind, wear English tweeds, read Henry James, and smoke a pipe. You want to blend in; you don't want to be a foreigner forever. Perhaps in some university town that would have been possible, but not in Chicago.

The city had an air of prosperity with all the banks, high-rise office buildings, and modern apartment houses along the lake, and yet it didn't feel like a big city. After eight o'clock in the evening, the Loop was dark except for a few movie houses and seedy bars. Hardly anyone was to be found on the streets on weeknights. Perhaps a few farmboys and drunken soldiers loitering outside the Greyhound bus station while the El passed overhead with a face or two pressed to its window, peeking into the dark. In winter it was even worse. There could be a bone-chilling wind blowing off the lake. At least working around the clock kept you warm.

Chicago gave a better sense of what America was than some small town or New York would have. Its mixture of being, at the same time, very modern and very provincial is a national characteristic. Add to that the realization that so much of our national prosperity depends on cheap labor. Immigrants and blacks kept Chicago humming.

I like the anarchy of the city. There were dives and strip joints a few blocks from the monumental Art Institute, with its magnificent collection of painting, and the ritzy hotels. Chicago was the garage sale of all the contradictions America could contain. A rusty water tower on the top of an old warehouse would look as beautiful as some architectural wonder along the lakeshore. Every notion of aesthetics one previously held had to be revised if one were to appreciate the city. My greatest teachers, in both art and literature, were the streets I roamed.

I graduated from high school in August of 1956 instead of June. I was missing some credits and had to take classes in summer school. I was supposed to go to college. My father was an optimist. He had bought the American Dream. It just hadn't been delivered yet. My father spent everything he earned and had accumulated large debts. Neither he nor my mother were very good at planning for the future. They never thought of finding out what colleges cost and what options were there. It didn't take me long to realize that I was on my own.

At the end of the summer I found a job as an office boy at the Chicago *Sun Times* and started attending night classes at the University of Chicago. I took the El to the city early in the morning and returned late at night. It was a lonely time. All my school friends were in college. And my parents were fighting all the time. The atmosphere was oppressive. I spent as little time as possible at home.

At the *Sun Times* I met a young writer, a fellow a little older than I, who had a furnished room on the North Side. That gave me an idea. I got a room too. It was in the basement of a tenement next to the hot-water boiler. The Oak Street beach, however, was only a few blocks away. I could go swimming any time I cared to. I went home early that night and told my parents I was moving out. They were stunned. For once they ganged up on me. I was too young, too inexperienced, and so on.

I couldn't be budged. I ended up yelling at them that I hated their fighting, couldn't bare the sound of their voices anymore. The next morning I was gone. Shortly after, my parents came to visit me, individually. They were appalled by the squalor I was living in. I didn't notice it. I was happy.

At work I was promoted to a proofreader, a union job. I made an excellent salary. I bought books and jazz records, and I painted. When I was broke I went home, or my father took me out to eat. Our relationship was fine once again. We did what we did best. We stayed out late drinking and talking.

I also made friends in the neighborhood and got to know some girls in the night school. Children of immigrants, sons and daughters of blue-collar workers, all set out to better themselves. The world of art, literature, philosophy, and sciences opened before us. I wanted to know everything instantly. Anytime I heard a name of a writer or a new idea, I would think: "Oh God, I'm completely ignorant! I better run to the library and look it up."

The public library downtown was the most exciting place in town. Incredibly, they'd let you take thick art books home so you could sit in your kitchen, eat your hot dogs and beans, and study the paintings of Giotto and Rembrandt. I took full opportunity of the library's beneficence. I read while riding the El to work; I read while pretending to shuffle papers on my desk; I read in bed and fell asleep with the lights still on.

By the time I arrived for the night classes the next day, I was dead tired. The classes were large, lively. There would always be one or two older students arguing with the teacher, saying things like: "Just because it's written in the book, it doesn't mean it's true." No matter how exhausted everybody happened to be, we all perked up watching the professor squirm.

A few people I encountered had ambitions in the arts, and that encouraged my own efforts. I painted more than I wrote, but poetry was my secret ambition. I was slowly getting hooked. In my neighborhood saloons, I met other budding writers. One of them introduced me to the poems of Lowell and Jarrell. Another gave me the work of Stevens and Pound. At night, when I was not attending classes, I went to the Newberry Library to read the French Surrealists and literary magazines. I even met the famous novelist Nelson Algren at a party.

The second time I bumped into him, I was carrying a volume of Robert Lowell's poetry. "Forget that," he told me. "A kid like you, just off the boat . . . Go read Whitman, read Sandburg and Vachel Lindsey." I took his advice.

The literary scene in Chicago was small. We'd all fit in a cold water flat, dark except for a couple of lit candles stuck in Chianti bottles and the obligatory Charlie Parker or Stan Getz on the cheap portable record player. The women mostly wore black. Their hair fell over their eyes so they gave one the impression they were playing peekaboo all the time. Parisian Left Bank existentialism had finally reached the shores of Lake Michigan. We were reading Sartre and Camus and quoting them to each other between puffs of cigarette smoke. There'd be a bottle of bad whiskey or cheap wine, but otherwise not much to eat or drink, since everybody was permanently broke.

In the literary crowd there were socialists and even a few ex-Communists. In those days, much more so than today, radical intellectuals came from working-class backgrounds. They worked with their hands, or they were union officials. Children of immigrants, they had plenty advice for a newcomer like me. Beware of the eastern literary establishment, they told me. If you don't watch out, you'll end up writing sonnets about Greek gods when you ought to be writing poems about old Polish ladies who sweep the downtown offices at night.

They had a point. When one is young and even more so when one is a foreigner, one is looking for role models. I wanted to blend in quickly. I was all ready to put on English tweeds with leather elbow patches and smoke a pipe, but they wouldn't let me. "Remember where you come from, kid," they reminded me time and time again. Thanks to them, I failed in my overwhelming desire to become a phony.

Even today I'm amazed by the change I underwent in that four- to five-year period. One moment, so it seemed, I was an unremarkable Yugoslav schoolboy, and the next moment I was on the midnight El riding to work. It's winter. It's bitter cold. Every time the door opens, we shiver, our teeth chatter. When it shuts, the heat turned on high, and our closely pressed bodies make it even worse. I'm asleep standing up. If I don't watch it, I'll miss my stop and wake up at the end of the line. I'll be halfway to Iowa. It'll be two in the morning, and I'll be the only one on the open platform pacing back and forth to keep warm while muttering to myself: "What a life! What a city! What a country!"

14

The streets are empty, it's raining, and my father and I are sitting in the Hotel Sherman bar listening to the bluesy piano. I'm not yet old enough to order a drink, but my father's presence is so authoritative and intimidating in his fine clothes that, when he orders for me too, the waiters do not dare ask about my age.

We talk. My father remembers a fly that would not let him sleep one summer fifty years ago. I tell him about an overcoat twice my size that my mother made me wear after the war. It was wintertime. People on the street would sometimes stop and watch me. The overcoat trailed the ground and made walking difficult. One day I was standing on the corner waiting to cross and I suppose looking miserable when a young woman gave me a small coin and walked away. I was terribly embarrassed.

"Was she pretty?" my father asked, laughing.

"Not at all," I assure him. "She looked like a hick, maybe a nun."

"A Serbian Ophelia," my father thinks.

And why not? Everything is possible.

Like when I told a young girl on the train to Chicago that I was a Russian. I described our apartment in Leningrad; the terrors of the long siege during the war; the death of my parents before a German firing squad, which we children had to witness; the hunger in DP camps in Europe; my grandmother who saw angels and painted icons. At some point, I had to run to the toilet and laugh out loud.

How much did she believe me? Who knows? Early in the morning, before getting off the train in Ohio, she gave me a long kiss in parting, which could have meant anything.

My first poems were published in the winter 1959 issue of the *Chicago Review*. They were written about a year and a half earlier. The two published poems differ a great deal. They don't seem to be written by the same poet. That was typical of my work at the time. I liked so many different kinds of poetry. One month I was a disciple of Hart Crane; the next month only Walt Whitman existed for me. When I fell in love with Pound I wrote an eighty-page-long poem on the Spanish Inquisition. It was awful, but the effort I put into it was tremendous. I'd work all night on it, go to work half-asleep, and then drag myself to night classes. I probably produced more poetry in the years 1956–61 than in all the years since. Except for a few poems, it was all bad, and one day I had the pleasure of destroying them all.

I was in the army, had been in the service for six months, when in the winter of 1962 I asked my father to send me the folder with the poems. I sat down on my cot the evening they arrived and read them. Everybody else in the barracks was shining shoes, playing cards, listening to their radios, and I was reading my collected poems. Perhaps being away from them for so long and being in such different circumstances made me see them clearly. I noticed all the obvious influences and awkward writing. There were at least a couple of hundred pages. I ripped them up in a hurry and threw them in the garbage. They embarrassed me. I still wanted to write poetry, but not that kind.

Now I look more affectionately on that Chicago period. Had I gone to college like everyone else, had I stayed at home with my parents, perhaps it wouldn't have turned out quite the way it did. Being alone like that, I had to justify my existence in my own eyes. It was obvious I wasn't going to succeed in life in the usual way, so I wrote and painted.

Otherwise, I had no idea what was to become of me. My previous life had taught me that making plans is a waste of time. My father used to ask me jokingly, "Where are we going to immigrate next?" The century's experiment in exile was still in progress. People like us were its laboratory animals. Strangest of all, one of the rats was writing poetry.

Even the old Romans knew. To have a son for a poet is bad news. I took precautions. I left home when I was eighteen. For the next couple of years I lived in a basement apartment next to a furnace that hissed and groaned as if it were about to explode any moment. I kept the windows open in all kinds of weather, figuring that way I'd be able to crawl out onto the sidewalk in a hurry. All winter long I wrote bad poems and painted bad pictures, wearing a heavy overcoat and gloves in that underground hole.

At the Chicago newspaper where I worked, I proofread obituaries and want ads. At night, I dreamed of lost dogs and funerals. Every payday I put a little money aside. One day I had enough to quit my job and take a trip to Paris, but I treated my friends to a smorgasbord in a fancy Swedish restaurant instead. It wasn't what we expected: there was too much smoked fish and pickled herring. After I paid the bill, everybody was still hungry, so we went down the street for pizza.

My friends wanted to know: When are you going to Paris? "I've changed my mind," I announced, ordering another round of beers. "I'm moving to New York, since I no longer have the money for Paris." The women were disappointed, but the fellows applauded. It didn't make sense, me going back to Europe after only being in the States for four years. Plus, to whom in Paris would I show my poems written in English?

"Your poems are just crazy images strung arbitrarily together," my pals complained, and I'd argue back: "Haven't you heard about surrealism and free association?" Bob Burleigh, my best friend, had a degree in English from the University of Chicago and possessed all the critical tools to do a close analysis of any poem. His verdict was: "Your poems don't mean anything."

My official reply to him was: "As long as they sound good, I'll keep them." Still, in private, I worried. I knew my poems were about something, but what was it? I couldn't define that "something" no matter how hard I tried. Bob and I would often quarrel about literature until the sun came up. To show him I was capable of writing differently, I wrote that eighty-page poem about the Spanish Inquisition. In the manner of Pound in his Cantos, I generously quoted original descriptions of tortures and public burnings. It wasn't surrealism, everybody agreed, but you still couldn't make heads or tails of what was going on. In one section I engaged Tomás de Torquemada in a philosophical discussion, just like Dostoyevsky's Ivan did with the Grand Inquisitor. I read the poem to a woman named Linda in a greasy spoon on Clark Street. When we ran to catch a bus, I left the poem behind. The next morning, the short-order cook and I tried to find it buried under the garbage out back. But it was a hot summer day, and the trash in the alley smelled bad and was thickly covered with flies. So we didn't look too closely.

Later, I stood at the corner where we had caught the bus the night before. I smoked a lot of cigarettes. I scratched my head. Several buses stopped, but I didn't get on any of them. The drivers would wait for me to make up my mind then give me a dirty look and drive off with a burst of speed and a parting cough of black smoke.

15

I left Chicago in August 1958 and went to New York, wearing a tan summer suit and a blue Hawaiian shirt.

The night of my farewell dinner, I got very drunk. At some point I went to the bathroom and could not find my way back. The restaurant was large and full of mirrors. I would see my friends seated in the distance, but, when I hurried toward them, I would come face-to-face with myself in the mirror. With the new beard I did not recognize myself immediately and almost apologized. In the end I gave up and sat down at an old man's table. He ate in silence, ignoring me, and I lit one of his cigarettes. Time passed. The place was emptying. The old man finally wiped his mouth with a napkin and pushed his full, untouched wineglass toward me. I would have stayed with him, if one of the women from our party hadn't found me and led me outside.

In New York the weather was hot and humid. The movie marquees on Forty-second Street were lit up twenty-four hours a day. Sailors were everywhere, and there were a few mounted policemen. I bought a long cigar and lit it nonchalantly for the benefit of a couple of young girls who stood at the curb afraid to cross the busy avenue.

A wino staggered up to me in Bryant Park and said: "I bark back at the dogs." A male hooker pulled a small statue of Jesus out of his tight pants and showed it to me. In Chinatown I saw a white hen pick a card with my fortune while dancing on a hot grill. In Central Park the early morning grass was matted where unknown lovers lay. In my motel room I kept the mirror busy by making stranger and stranger faces at myself.

"Sweetheart," a husky woman's voice said to me when I answered the phone at four in the morning. I hung up immediately. It was incredibly hot, so I slept naked. My only window was open, but there was a brick wall a few feet outside of it and no draft. I suspected there were rats on the wall, but I had no choice.

Late mornings I sat in a little luncheonette on Eighth Street reading the sports pages or writing poems:

> In New York on 14th Street
> Where peddlers hawk their wares
> And cops look the other way,
> There you meet the eternal—
> Con artists selling watches, silk ties, umbrellas,
> After nightfall
> When the cross-town wind blows cold
> And my landlady throws a skinny chicken
> In the pot to boil. Fumes rise.
> I can draw her ugly face on the kitchen window,
> Then take a quick peek at the street below.

It was still summer. On the advice of my mother, I went to visit an old friend of hers. She served me tea and cucumber sandwiches and asked about my plans for the future. I replied that I had no idea. I could see that she was surprised. To encourage me, she told me about someone who knew at the age of ten that he wanted to be a doctor and was now studying at a prestigious medical school. I agreed to come to a dinner where I would meet a number of brilliant young men and women my age and profit by their example. Of course, I failed to show up.

At the Phoenix Book Shop in the Village, I bought a book of French stories. It was on sale and very cheap, but even so I only had enough money left to buy myself a cup of coffee and a toasted English muffin. I took my time sipping the lukewarm coffee and nibbling my muffin as I read the book. It was a dark and rainy night. I walked the near-empty streets for hours in search of the two people I knew in the city. Not finding them home, I returned to my room, crawled shivering under the covers, and read in the silence, interrupted only by the occasional wailing of an ambulance:

Monsieur Lantin had met the girl at a party given one evening by his office superior, and love had caught him in its net. She was the daughter of a country tax collector who had died a few years before. She had come to Paris then with her mother, who struck up acquaintance with a few middle-class families in her district in the hope of marrying her off. They were poor and decent, quiet and gentle. The girl seemed the perfect example of a virtuous woman to whom every sensible young man dreams of entrusting his life. Her simple beauty had a modest, angelic charm, and the imperceptible smile that always hovered about her lips seemed to be a reflection of her heart.

After midnight my hotel was quiet as a tomb. I had to play the radio real low with my ear brushing against it in the dark. "Clap your hands, here comes Charlie," some woman sang, a hot Dixieland band backing her up, but just then I didn't think it was very funny.

While the weather was still good, I sat on benches in Washington Square Park or Central Park, watching people and inventing stories to go along with their faces. If I was wearing my only suit and it rained, I sat in the lobbies of big hotels smoking cigars. I went window-shopping almost every night. An attractive pair of shoes or a shirt would make me pay a return visit even after midnight. The movies consumed an immense amount of my time. I would emerge after seeing the double feature twice, dazed, disoriented, and hungry. I often had a toothache and waited for days for it to go away. I typed with two fingers on an ancient Underwood typewriter that woke my hotel neighbors. They'd knock on my walls until I stopped. On a Monday morning while everyone else was rushing off to work, I took a long subway ride to Far Rockaway. Whenever the subway came out of the ground, I would get a glimpse of people working in offices and factories. I could tell they were hot and perspiring. On the beach there were only a few bathers, seemingly miles apart.

When I stretched out on the sand and looked up, the sky was empty and blue. When I was on the way home late one night, a drunk came out of a dark doorway with a knife in hand. He swayed and couldn't say what he wanted. I ran. Even though I knew there was no chance he would catch up with me, I didn't stop for many blocks. When I finally did, I no longer knew where I was. Around that time I wrote:

> Purse-snatchers
> Keep away from poor old women
> They yell the loudest.
> Stick to young girls,
> The dreamy newlyweds
> Buying heart-shaped pillows for their beds.
> Bump into a drunk instead,
> Offer a pencil to sell.
> When he pulls out a roll of bills,
> Snatch all he's got and split.
> Duck that nightstick
> Or your ears will ring
> Even in your coffin.

I am only mildly exaggerating when I say that I couldn't take a piss without a book in my hand. I read to fall asleep and to wake up. I read at my various jobs, hiding the book among the papers on my desk or in the half-open drawer. I read everything from Plato to Mickey Spillane. Even in my open coffin, some day, I should be holding a book. *The Tibetan Book of the Dead* would be the most appropriate, but I'd prefer a sex manual or the poems of Emily Dickinson.

The book that made all the difference to my idea of poetry was an anthology of contemporary Latin American verse that I bought on Eighth Street. Published by New Directions in 1942 and long out of print by the time I bought my copy, it introduced me to the poems of Jorge Luis Borges, Pablo Neruda, Jorge Carrera Andrade, Drummond de Andrade, Nicholas Guillen, Vincente Huidobro, Jorge de Lima, César Vallejo, Octavio Paz, and so many others. After that anthology, the poetry I read in literary magazines struck me as pretty timid. Nowhere in the *Sewanee Review* or the *Hudson Review* could I find poems like "Biography for the Use of the Birds" or "Liturgy of My Legs" or this one by the Haitian poet Emile Roumer, "The Peasant Declares His Love":

High-yellow of my heart, with breasts like tangerines,
you taste better to me than eggplant stuffed with crabs,
you are the tripe in my pepper pot,
the dumpling in my peas, my tea of aromatic herbs.
You're the corned beef whose customhouse is my heart,
my mush with syrup that trickles down the throat.
You're a steaming dish, mushroom cooked with rice,
crisp potato fried, and little fresh fish fried brown . . .
My hankering for love follows wherever you go.
Your bum is a gorgeous basket brimming with fruits and meats.
(From *Anthology of Contemporary Latin-American Poetry,* edited by
Dudley Fitts [New Directions, 1942]503)

The folk surrealism, the mysticism, the eroticism, and the wild flights of romance and rhetoric in these poets were much more appealing to me than what I found among the French and German modernists whom I already knew. Of course, I started imitating the South Americans immediately:

I'm the last offspring of the old raven
Who fed himself on the flesh of the banged . . .
A dark nest full of old misfortunes,
The wind raging above the burning treetops,
A cold north wind looking for its bugle.

I was reading Jacob Bohme in the New York Public Library on Forty-second Street on a hot, muggy morning when a woman arrived in what must have been last night's party dress. She was not much older than I was, but the hour and lack of sleep gave her a world-weary air. She consulted the catalog, filled out a slip, received her book, and sat down at a table across from mine. I craned my neck, I squinted in my nearsighted way, and I even brushed past her a couple of times, but I could not figure out what she was reading. The book had no pictures, and it wasn't poetry, but she was so absorbed that her hair fell into her eyes. Perhaps she was sleeping.

Then, all of a sudden, when I was absolutely sure she was snoozing away, she turned a page with a long, thin finger. Her fingers were too thin, in my opinion. Was the poor dear eating properly? Was she dying of consumption? Her breasts in her low-cut black dress, on the other hand, looked pretty healthy. I saw no problem there.

Did she notice my spying on her? Absolutely not, unless she was a consummate actress, a budding Gene Tierney.

Of all the people I watched surreptitiously over the years, how many noticed me and still remember me the way I remember them? I just have to close my eyes, and there she is, still reading her mysterious book. I don't see myself and have no idea what I look like or what clothes I'm wearing. The same goes for everyone else in the large reading room. They have no faces; they do not exist. She's reading slowly and turning pages carefully. The air is heavy and muggy, and the ceiling fan doesn't help. It could be a Monday or a Tuesday, July or August. I'm not even certain if it was 1959 or 1960.

I went to hear Alan Tate read his poems at New York University. There were no more than twenty of us all together: a few friends of the poet, a couple of English professors, a scattering of graduate students, and one or two oddballs like me seated way in the back. Tate was thin and dapper, polite, and read in what I suppose could be described as a cultivated Southern voice. I had already read some of his essays and liked them very much, but the poetry, because of its seriousness and literary sophistication, was tedious. You would have to be nuts to want to write like that, I thought, remembering Jorge de Lima's poem in which he describes God tattooing the virgin: "Come, let us read the virgin, let us learn the future . . . / O men of little sight." Not a spot on her skin without tattoos: "that is why the virgin is so beautiful," the Brazilian poet says.

I'm packing parcels in the Lord & Taylor basement during the Christmas rush with a bunch of losers. One fellow is an inventor. He has a new kind of aquarium with piped music, which makes it look as if the fish are doing water ballet, every goldfish an Esther Williams, but the world is not interested. Another man supports three ex-wives, so he has a night job in addition to this one. His eyes fall shut all the time. He's so pale, he could pass for a stiff in an open coffin.

Then there's Felix, a mousy fellow a bit older than I who

claims to be a distant relative of the English royal family. One time he brought the chart of his family tree to make us stop making fun of him and see the truth. What did not make sense was his poverty. He said he was a writer but wouldn't tell us what kind. "Are you writing porno?" one tough Puerto Rican girl asked him.

Her name was Rosie. She liked boxing. One time she and I went on a date to watch the fights at the Garden. We sat in the Spanish section. "Kill the bastard," she screamed all evening. At the end she was so tired of shouting she wouldn't even have a drink with me and had to rush home.

At one of the readings at NYU given by a now forgotten academic poet of the 1950s, just as the professional lovers of poetry in the audience were already closing their eyes blissfully in anticipation of the poet's familiar, soul-stirring clichés, there was the sound of paper being torn. We all turned around to look. A shabby old man was ripping newspapers into a brown shopping bag. He saw people glare at him and stopped. The moment we turned back to the poet, who went on reading, oblivious to everything, in a slow monotone, the man resumed ripping, but now more cautiously, with long pauses between rips.

And so it went: the audience would turn around with angry faces, he'd stop for a while and then continue, while the poet read on and on.

After several fleabag hotels, I finally found a home at Hotel Albert on Tenth Street and University Place. The room was small, and of course the window faced a brick wall, but the location was perfect, and the rent was not too high. From Friday noon to Sunday morning I had plenty of money. The rest of the week, I scraped by on candy bars for lunch and hamburgers or cheap Chinese food for dinner. Later I would buy a glass of beer for fifteen cents and spend the rest of the night making it last forever.

Publications of my poems came slowly. Every day the mail brought me another rejection slip. One, I remember, had a personal note from the editor that said: "Dear Mr. Simic, you're obviously an intelligent young man, so why do you waste your time writing so much about pigs and cockroaches?"

To spit on guys like you, I wanted to write back.

After work on Fridays my friend Jim Brown and I would tour the bars. We'd start with a few beers at the Cedar Tavern, near our rooms, then walk over to the San Remo on MacDougal Street, where Brown would have a martini and I would drink red wine. Afterward, we would most likely go to the White Horse, where Brown had a tab, to drink whiskey. With some of the regulars, Brown would discuss everything from socialism to old movies; I didn't open my mouth much, for, the moment I did and people heard my accent, I would have to explain where I came from and how, and why. I thought of printing a card, the kind deaf panhandlers pass around, with my abbreviated life story on it and an abbreviated account of the geography and history of the Balkans.

Around midnight Brown and I would walk back to Cedar, which was packed by then, and have a nightcap. Over hamburgers Brown would harangue me for not having read Rabelais or Sir Thomas Browne yet. Later, lying in my bed, with drink and talk floating in my head and the sound of creaking beds, smokers' coughs, and love cries coming from the other rooms, I would not be able to sleep. I would go over the interesting and stupid things I had heard that night.

For instance, in those days there were still true believers around who idealized the life in the Soviet Union and disparaged the United States. What upset me the most was when some nice-looking young woman would nod in agreement. I reproached myself for not telling her how people over there were turned into angels at the point of a gun. My shyness and cowardice annoyed me no end. I couldn't fall asleep for hours, and then, just as I was finally drifting off, one of my rotten teeth would begin a little chat with me.

"You look like a young Franz Schubert," the intense-looking woman told me as we were introduced.

At that same party I spoke to a lawyer who insisted we had met in London two years before. I explained my accent to a medical student by telling him that I was raised by a family of deaf mutes.

There was a girl, too, who kept smiling sweetly at me without saying a word. Her mother told me that I reminded her of her brother, who was executed by the Nazis in Norway. She was going to give me more details, but I excused myself, announcing to everyone that I had a sudden and terrible toothache that required an immediate visit to the drugstore.

16

Sweet and lovely lady be good . . . I'm lost in this great big city.
Won't you please have a little pity?

—Ira and George Gershwin

"That thing came from a maximum security penitentiary," she
told me.

I could not say what kind of metal it was made of or what it
had originally been used for. Part of a rusty machine, some kind
of pin. I touched it with my tongue and was surprised by how
cold it felt. Like the stone floor in the solitary, I thought.

"One writes the years of one's imprisonment with such an
object," I said.

"One must keep it hidden at all times," she replied with an air
of mystery.

The man who left it with her was her lover for a month. That
had been some years earlier.

"He used to scratch my back at night with it," she told me.

She wore a flowered silk robe and red slippers on her bare
feet. They kept falling off when she crossed her legs. I still held
the metal object in my hand. I kept wondering if she would give
it to me if I asked for it, if I pretended to beg.

Her robe was slightly open. I put the object on the table
between us. Outside it was beginning to rain. She jumped to
close the windows, giving me a peek, in the process, of her
breasts and her long legs. Soon it was raining so hard the room
grew dark.

She talked, and I listened.

"I have the impression," she said to me, "that in my life there
have been more nights than days. It was like night came, and
then, just as the new day was about to break, another would
follow immediately in its wake."

"I forget the face of my lovers because it has always been night. Only their bodies still keep their ghostly whiteness for me. I just want to touch them, but I no longer have the right."

Just before I left she turned on a single table lamp to read me a poem, the plot of which I still remember.

In the woods one Sunday, when they were children, she and her brother came upon a couple lying on the ground. Hand in hand, afraid themselves of being lost, they saw what they first surmised was a patch of snow. In a spot rarely visited, with the wind sighing over the new leaves, they came upon the embraced ones, the two naked people clutching each other on the cold ground. It was spring. The woods had already a bit of purple shade. There was a bird, too, singing and falling silent as they stole by.

It was still raining when I came out on the street. I was still twenty years old, and she was at least forty. Our connection was poetry, which we both wrote and showed to each other. I stopped by her place in late afternoons, often unannounced. It was all very simple. I was attracted to her, I also liked her stories, so I came. Otherwise, I knew nothing about her, except that she grew up in some place like Minnesota or Montana and that she had lived in Europe for a long time. She had the tired eyes and faded beauty of someone whose life has had many ups and downs. She could've been a rich expatriate living alone and drinking heavily in some villa in Florence. She could've been a nightclub singer of another era. In any case, she was always alone, letting me visit for hours and then, without a warning, throwing me out, supposedly just remembering that someone was coming to see her or that she had an appointment to keep.

A couple of times I spied on her from across the street. The first time she went out in a great hurry, wearing a wide-brimmed hat and dark glasses, and caught a cab on the corner. The next time she didn't come out at all. A small boy with glasses entered her brownstone and then a young couple carrying grocery bags. At ten her lights were still on, so I crossed the street and found the doors unlocked. I went up without a thought in my head, only a powerful desire to see her. On the third floor I put my ear to her door. There was not a sound to be heard. I wanted to knock, I should've knocked, but instead I stood there, listening to my heart beat wildly. After a long wait, I went home.

Next door to where I lived on East Thirteenth Street, there was a rundown brownstone with a basement from which a street vendor supplier operated. Derelicts, if they were hired, sold umbrellas, ties, fake Swiss watches, miracle potato peelers, and other such junk, up and down Fourteenth Street. The boss looked like Anthony Quinn's Zampano, the circus artist who breaks heavy chains in *La Strada*. He examined his men in the morning and chased away the ones who appeared too shabby, too sickly, or who were simply too drunk. Every time he noticed me watching, he gave me a nasty look that said, "I'm going to wring your neck kid, one of these days!"

In the evening, and even late into the night, he'd be there outside his establishment, eyeing me evilly as I went by. I attributed my strange dreams to his presence.

I dreamed, for instance, that I was in a dressing room of some kind. It could've been vaudeville, a strip joint, a circus, or perhaps a sports arena. The mirrors had cracks in them, and the sofa had its stuffing showing. I suspected there were wrestlers, dancers, acrobats, and transvestites about to return. When she walked in, I was very surprised. She wore a low-cut black dress with thin straps and did not appear to see me. She lay down on the sofa, and her eyes closed as if she were extremely, hopelessly tired. As I drew close, the powerful reality of her body in my dream surprised me even more. I, who had never seen her naked, felt in that instant before waking that I knew her arms, legs, and mouth as if I had covered them with kisses many times.

After one such dream I wrote a poem that I still vaguely recollect. In a field next to the town dump a man and a woman sit drinking until the heat makes them take their clothes off. There's an old tub thrown in the tall weeds where she goes to sit and pretends to wash herself. The man dances around her playing the wine bottle as if it were a goatherd's flute. When some birds fly over them, she throws her head back, so that her breasts bounce in full view above the rusty rim of the tub. He, meanwhile, is sitting on the ground, looking for the thorn in his feet, his cock stiff between his hairy legs.

I called the poem "Pastoral" and thought of showing it to her but never summoned the courage to, telling myself that it was not very good, that it was incomprehensible and kind of embarrassing.

She had a cousin who counted leaves all day long, she told me. He was mad, and they had plenty of trees. After a while he'd grow tired and would sit on the ground, his finger still pointing up, his lips still moving. It was hard to tell one leaf from another with the night coming, he confided to her once. She imagined a figure with many zeros lengthening in his head like a comet's tail. While she was telling me this, she kept looking at me with a little smile as if I were her mad cousin.

On another occasion she told me how her mother liked walking barefoot in the rain. Everyone on the street would run for cover and stand in doorways watching her take off her shoes and stockings in plain view with the rain pouring down. They'd stroll together barefoot, kicking the puddles with all those disapproving faces watching.

Where was that? I wanted to know, but just then, and for the first time, she asked me to stay for dinner. She would make squid and rice, and I would help her. I told her that I was crazy about squid and rice. And it was true. When it came to food, music, books, I was pretty sophisticated. In everything else I was a lost sheep in the woods.

Since I'm writing this thirty years later, I'm more aware and less embarrassed about my shyness then. I remember watching her clean the squid, expertly removing the delicate, finlike bones. I stood right behind her. Her hands were surprisingly ugly. The fingernails appeared bitten and viciously at that. Strong, brutal hands so much in contrast with the back of her neck, which was white and soft. I thought of the girls who sat in front of me in grade school bending over their exams. I was so close, my lips lightly brushing her pale blond hair; I'm astonished I didn't kiss her.

I can still relive that moment with undiminished clarity. I can still peek down her robe and see her full breasts down to their nipples. She was now chopping onions; tears were running down her face. She was laughing and explaining to me the Spanish peasant recipe she was using as I hovered over her.

Is that why she always had that little smile for me? She knew, of course, what was going on in my head and in my pants, and that was the fun of it for her.

Later, over wine and cheese, I showed her a poem I had just written. It was not the one about the naked lady in a tub. It went like this:

> The Holy Virgin lives over the grocery store.
> She wears a Salvation Army uniform even when she
> > Steps out to throw the garbage out.
> Mice scurry around her feet.
> St. John the Baptist has a pigeon coop on the roof.
> His martyrdom includes emptying bedpans in a hospital.
> One night he knocks on her door and walks right in.
> There's a dressmaker's dummy to greet him,
> Ugly little pins stuck in it.
> She is lying in bed with her eyes closed.
> The room is dark; the sky is windy and cloudy.
> Her eyes are still tightly closed.

Before she had time to comment on my awkward blasphemy, the phone rang in the next room, she answered it, and told me I must leave immediately because she had to go out.

That night I woke with a huge hard-on. I wanted to go over to her place. I was absolutely certain in that moment that she was expecting me to do just that. Her door would open even before I would touch it. It'd be pitch dark. She'd lead me by the hand, and I wouldn't make a sound, even with her naked body brushing against me and her hand gripping mine so hard. We'd be like two blind people, two blind lovers in an unfamiliar world.

I dressed quickly and, without tying my shoes, ran into the street. It was long past midnight. The streets were empty, and the summer night was warm and humid. Her windows were dark, her front door locked. I sat on the steps, tied my shoelaces, and had a smoke. Since I was not in the mood for bed, I took a walk. Dark streets, dark trees, but then up ahead in the next block there was noise and lights. A party was in progress; the crowd had even spilled onto the sidewalk. The guests were dressed as if they had gone to a wedding or the opera. They were in high spirits.

I did not hesitate. I walked right in. The entrance was packed like a rush-hour subway. I had to squeeze from room to room, from floor to floor. Everybody was busy talking, and nobody was paying attention to me. I wanted a drink, but I couldn't find the bar. I opened a wrong door and found a white-haired man in a tuxedo puking in the toilet. I opened another and found a black Labrador tied to the radiator in a room no bigger than a closet. He was happy to see me. I would not have minded staying with him, but all of a sudden I had a hunch that she might be there at the party.

Again, I looked everywhere. I even got to the roof, where I found a couple tottering and kissing close to the edge. Finally, I asked a drunken woman everybody called Marilyn where the drinks were coming from. She handed over a bottle of Irish whiskey without saying a word. She was with an older man who kept whispering in her ear and giving me unfriendly looks. I took the bottle into the living room and pushed my way into the corner. I stood there drinking and watching the people. I had no idea who they were or what the occasion was, and I didn't care. The women seemed uncommonly beautiful. They were all accompanied. Their escorts made them titter or gaze at them with endless admiration.

They should all be in bed screwing, I thought. I was drinking heavily and expecting her to come into view. "We'll fuck right here on the floor," I told a neighbor. The fellow gave me a wary look. I said it again louder. "I'm going to take my clothes off right now so I'm ready when she arrives," I warned him. More people were watching me now. I was already unbuttoning my shirt and loosening up my belt.

"It's him," someone shouted, and they all looked in another direction. Someone had just arrived, and they were all waving to him. It seemed he could only stay for a short time. I couldn't even see the man, but he was obviously a big deal. Suddenly, I felt very tired. I sat on the floor, took another long swig out of the bottle, and closed my eyes. I still had the lovely premonition that she'd come. She'd touch my cheek, letting her long red nails scratch me a little. I'd open my eyes and greet that little smile of hers with a little smile of my own.

I counted to a hundred very slowly, then to another hundred, even more slowly.

"You must leave now," said the black maid who woke me. I obeyed instantly. The living room was empty, and so were the stairs. On the street there was the hush of early Sunday morning; at home, a mouse dead in the kitchen trap with a tiny trickle of blood out of its mouth.

I waited a week. I went to my job selling dress shirts at Stern's Department Store on Forty-second Street. I wore a shirt and tie myself and was always expected to be extremely polite with customers. Men were no problem, but the women drove me nuts. I'd show them a shirt, and they'd notice a nonexistent spot on the collar. I'd show them another, but the spot would be somewhere else. If I talked back, they'd complain to the manager, who'd chew me out in front of them even though he knew I was right.

In the evening I made the round of local saloons to find my friend Sal and complain about women.

"Perfect creatures," Sal replied every time. He loved them all and refused to entertain the slightest disparagement of the female sex.

Somebody at the bar would object, mentioning some sourpuss in the neighborhood. "How about her?"

A real bitch, everybody would agree.

"She just needs the right kind of loving," was Sal's opinion. He thought the *Kama Sutra* should be read to little children. As for my difficulties with Miss X, he told me over and over again that I was a complete jerk.

The afternoon I was to make my last visit to the house on West Twelfth Street, I carried a bottle of French wine and a can of pâté. I had just gotten some money from my father and was in a jaunty mood. I expected us to sit and drink as always. Billie Holiday or Lester Young would be playing on the phonograph with the sound turned down low. "Blue Lester" or "Lady Be Good," perhaps. The night would slowly come, and she would turn on the lights. I would change records, picking out the saddest songs. We'd listen to "Moanin' Low" and "Mean to Me," and the night would fall. I would come over to where she was sitting and bury my head between her legs. Or I'd wait till we couldn't see each other and tell her I loved her. I felt reckless and giddy with confidence.

The front door was unlocked, so I ran upstairs two steps at a time and knocked. There was no answer, so I banged on the door with my fist. Finally, I heard heavy steps, the door opened, and a man who appeared to have been sleeping stood there. He was my age. He even looked like me. His T-shirt, I remember, was wet with sweat. He didn't say anything. He expected me to say something, and I just muttered an apology and quickly walked downstairs.

I never went back, though I meant to. I have no idea to this day who the woman was or the man who opened the door. I looked for her name in literary journals over the years, but I never found her. I thought of her recently, walking on West Twelfth Street. It reminded me that I still have a part of a poem she wrote. It's typed on the stationery of Hotel Drake, Chicago, and has just these eight lines:

> Whoever has faith in love
> And goes wherever her feet take her
> In the evening crowd,
> Hoping to be tapped on the shoulder
> By a stranger, whispering already,
> I must tell you of the many things
> That lie heavy on my heart
> Of which I have kept silent so long . . .

The rest of the poem I lost moving from New York to San Francisco many years ago.

17

In the days of my youth, I could get a good night's sleep on a hard floor without a cover. I'd stretch on my back fully dressed, shut my eyes, and drift off immediately. That's how I slept in prison in Yugoslavia when I was ten years old. I still have a dim memory of the crowded floor of the cell, the men sleeping squeezed together and me awake sitting up in the milky light of the new day. What were my thoughts then? Was I afraid? Hungry? Cold? I wore shorts when we were caught crossing the border. My legs were badly scratched from crawling through the thick woods at night. What gave my mother the courage to set out like that with two small boys and two strange men as guides into the dark? I'd like to ask her, but she's been dead for years. I imagine her rolling her eyes in exasperation. By the time she was eighty-nine, she was convinced that nothing that happened to her in her life made any sense. Bombs falling out of the blue sky, cities in smoke, corpses lying individually or in heaps everywhere you looked, and here I'm still asking for an explanation.

A dog will join you on the floor, even a cat, but rarely a human being. Monastic cells, solitary confinement, sleeping in the open, and sidewalks of big cities where homeless huddle are what come to mind. The hard surface is good for your spine, people tell you. I had my doubts. A woman locked me out of her apartment once. Pissed, tired, and tipsy, I went to sleep right in front of her door using her doormat as a pillow. I woke hours later to catch sight of an old woman walking past me with her little dog, who gave me a look of understanding. Even passionate screwing on the floor has a way of coming to an abrupt end the instant you realize your knees or your back are killing you. That morning I rose quickly and hurried after the old woman and her dog.

Rest during the day so you can sleep well at night.

—Ancestral wisdom

There were periods in my life when I couldn't remember a single dream. I went around embarrassed, trying to imagine what dreaming would be like. At other times I found myself every night with a different cast of characters dressed like guests at a funeral. More freaks packed into one dream than in all the sideshows in the world. I acted in many tragedies and porn flicks. The sets and the lighting were those of a 1920s German expressionist movie. There was a lot of shadow where further dangers lurked. The sky in my dreams was always overcast. I was in some vaguely familiar city where, for some reason, I could not give my terrors a slip. Everyone must have walked on padded feet, because there was never any sound.

I dreamed of a school of insomnia where I studied hard in the back seat of an empty classroom.

I dreamed of a lollipop in the shape of a skull.

I dreamed of my father on his knees nibbling wildflowers.

Once I permitted myself to be fired from a cannon.

Everyone I met looked younger, even the dead.

I dreamed of a woman picking my pocket in the street, and that woman was Veronica Lake.

I dreamed of the silence of the Sahara Desert.

Have researches ever been made into the wretched loneliness of the dreamer?

This beast loves to be lied to.

On the night of February 7, 1959, I dreamed I was Stalin's secretary. I walked around with adoring countenance, terribly afraid and at the same time ashamed of myself.

I dreamed of a monkey with a rosary.

I dreamed I barked back at a dog.

Fairy-tale stuff . . . like eating soup with a pin.

It was like watching myself through dark glasses on a rainy evening.

I dreamed I was naked with M. on the crowded subway, and she wanted me to make love to her.

I found myself inexplicably in the same seaside hotel again and again embracing the hips and moist sex of a woman whose face I could not see.

A Chinese monastery in the mist—what the hell was I doing there?

Were these the scenes of the future life or the consequences of eating a large pepperoni pizza at bedtime?

Truth is either what can be communicated or what has no hope of ever being communicated.

Dreams, you're as dumb and unintelligible as history!

My happiness was just around the corner, and so was my death.

I fell off buildings repeatedly. I tried to flap my arms in a hurry or hold myself back by grabbing my head by the ears, but it was no use.

And I've never even seen the moon in dreams!

I would not have been the same man if I had been able to sleep well in my life.

It all started when I was twelve. I fell in love. I lay in the dark trying to imagine what was under her black skirt. I thought her name was Maria, but it was really Insomnia.

In a life full of troubles, Insomnia kept me company against the fear of the dark.

We were like young lovers. I had no secrets from her. Our silences were as eloquent as our speech.

Most of the time, I resisted the impulse to toss and turn. I didn't blink. I tried not to swallow. I didn't even move my tongue.

My mind was like Ulysses. We took long sea voyages. We were often in South Seas and China. In nineteenth-century London and St. Petersburg we were afraid.

Mostly, though, we were calm. Like Noah's crow, we reconnoitered our galaxy. Acrobats of the abyss, face-to-face with the ineffable.

We had conversations with old philosophers, mystics, and death camp prisoners.

"I'm awake because I don't wish to be surprised by my future," said one.

"There's freedom only for the awake," said another.

Horror of consciousness, everybody's favorite home movie.

I often felt like a schoolboy condemned to write the same word or two over and over and over again on the blackboard.

My shoes with their broken and reknotted laces stayed in the corner.

Time vanished. Drunk with its own special brand of melancholy, eternity came to breathe on me.

My fleas don't sleep well either.

Occasionally, I climb my own private stairway to the darkest corner of the sky. It is like an empty nightclub with a tragic menu placed on each table.

The child I was often came to visit me. He wanted to show me things in a theater with mice-eaten red curtains. I went reluctantly, since, of course, he didn't exist. I could've been walking backward on a tightrope with eyes closed.

At 3 A.M. I always believed the worst. Lying stiffly, counting my heartbeats to a thousand and one!

I pretended to believe in the future, but, even so, I had fits of doubts. Even when I slept soundly, I dreamed I was awake.

My conscience knew its business. I was continuously under its close surveillance. I had a theory: God is afraid of insomniacs, but not the devil.

My love read Victorian novels at night, while I read mysteries and history books. The rustle of our pages being turned made mice in the walls tremble; the angel of death put on his thick glasses to peek over our shoulders.

So many judges, so little justice in the world! Murder is a folk art, it occurred to me in my fiftieth. They kept perfecting it without ever being pleased with the results.

"Long live the brotherhood of the sleepless!" I shouted with the noose tightening around my neck, but all anyone else heard was the old bedsprings sigh and creak.

And then, just as the day was breaking, I smiled to myself, as I felt my love leaving my side.

18

My next job was in the Doubleday Bookstore on Fifth Avenue. I would read on the sly while the manager was busy elsewhere. Eventually, I could guess what most of the customers wanted even before they opened their mouths. There were the best-seller types and self-help book types, the old ladies in love with mysteries, and sensitive young women who were sure to ask for Kahil Gibran's *The Prophet.*

But I didn't like standing around all day, so I got a job addressing the labels at New York University Press. After a while they hired my friend Sal to give me help. We sat in the back room playing chess for hours on end. Occasionally, one of the editors would come and ask us to pick up his dry cleaning, pay an electric bill, and buy a sandwich or a watermelon.

Sal and I took our time. We sat in the park and watched the girl students go by. Sal was a few years older than I and a veteran of the air force. When he was just a teenager, his parents died suddenly, and he inherited the family bakery in Brooklyn. He got married and in two years had managed to ruin the family business.

How? I wanted to know.

"I took my wife to the Latin Quarter and Copacabana every night," he told me, with obvious satisfaction. He joined the air force to flee his creditors. Now he was a veteran and a home-spun philosopher.

Sal agreed with H. L. Mencken that you are as likely to find an honest politician as you are an honest burglar. Only the church, in his view, was worse: "The priests are all perverts," he confided to me, "and the pope is the biggest pervert of all."

"What about Billy Graham?" I asked, trying not to drop my watermelon.

"That's all he thinks about," Sal assured me with a wink.

The military was no better in his view. All the officers he had met were itching to commit mass murder. Even Ike, in his opinion, had the mug of a killer.

Only women were good. "If you want to have a happy life," he told me every day, "learn to get along with the ladies."

With the arrival of the Beats, both as a literary movement and as a commercial venture, the scene changed. Coffee shops sprang up everywhere in the Village. In addition to folk singing and comedy acts, they offered poetry readings. "Where the Beat Meet the Elite," said a banner over a tourist trap. "Oh God, come down and fuck me!" some young woman prayed in her poem, to the horror of out-of-town customers.

But New York was also a great place for poetry: within the same week, one could also hear John Berryman and May Swenson, Allen Ginsberg and Denise Levertov, Frank O'Hara and LeRoi Jones. I went to readings for two reasons: to hear the poets and to meet people. I could always find, sitting grumpily in the corner, someone with whom it was worth striking up a conversation. The readings themselves left me with mixed feelings. One minute I would be dying of envy and the next of boredom and contempt. It took me a few years to sort it all out. In the meantime, I sought other views. I'd spot someone thumbing an issue of the *Black Mountain Review* in the Eighth Street Bookstore and end up talking to them. Often that would lead to a cup of coffee or a beer. No matter how hip you think you are, someone always knows more. The literary scene had a greater number of true originals then than it has today. There was Tony, an unemployed bricklayer, who went around saying things like: "Even the mutes are unhappy since they've learned to read lips."

Then there was the tall, skinny fellow with graying hair I talked to after hearing Richard Wilbur read at NYU. He told me that the reason contemporary poets were so bad was because they were lazy. I asked what he meant, and he explained: "They write a couple of hours per week, and the rest of the time they have a ball living in the lap of luxury with rich floozies hanging on their arms and paying their bills. You've got to write sixteen hours per day to be a great poet." I asked him what he did, and he muttered that he worked in the post office.

During one of my rare trips back to Chicago to visit my mother, Bob Burleigh told me about a terrific young poet I ought to meet. His name was Bill Knott. He worked nights in a hospital emptying bedpans and was usually home during the day. He lived in a rooming house not too far away, so we went to see him.

An old woman answered the bell and said Bill was upstairs in his room. But when we knocked there was no answer. Bob shouted, "It's me Bob." Just as we were about to leave, I heard a sound of many bottles clinking together, and the door opened slowly. Soon we saw what it was: we had to wade through an ankle-deep layer of Pepsi bottles to advance into the room. Bill was a large man in a dirty white T-shirt; one lens of his glasses was wrapped with masking tape, presumably broken. The furnishings were a bed with a badly stained mattress, a large poster of Monica Vitti, a refrigerator with an old TV set on it, and a couple of chairs and a table with piles of books on them. Books sat on the bed, and I was given a chair after Bill swept some books on the floor. Bill, who hadn't sat down, asked us: "How about a Pepsi?" "Sure," we replied. "What the heck!" The fridge, it turned out, contained nothing but rows and rows of Pepsi bottles.

We sipped our sodas and talked poetry. Bill had read everything: we spoke of René Char, and Bill quoted Char from memory. Regarding contemporary American poetry, we were in complete agreement: except for Robert Bly, James Wright, Frank O'Hara, and a few others, the poets we read in the magazines were the most unimaginative, dull, pretentious, know-nothing bunch you were ever likely to encounter. As far as these poets were concerned, Arthur Rimbaud, Hart Crane, and Guillaume Apollinaire might never have existed. They knew nothing of modern art, cinema, and jazz. We had total contempt for them. We bought magazines like *Poetry* in those days in order to nourish our rage: Bob and I regularly analyzed its poems so we could grasp the full range of their imbecility. I did not see any of Bill Knott's poems that day, but later he became one of my favorite poets.

Back in New York, I had a long talk with Robert Lowell about nineteenth-century French poetry. We were at a party following some reading at the Y. It was late, and most people had gone home. Lowell was seated in an armchair, two young women were sitting on the floor, one on each side of him, and I was on the floor facing him. Although he spoke interestingly about Charles Baudelaire, Tristan Corbière, and Jules Laforgue, what had me totally captivated were not his words but his hands. Early in our conversation he massaged the women's necks; after a while he slid his hands down inside their dresses and massaged their breasts. They didn't seem to mind, hanging on his every word. Why wasn't I a great poet? Instead of joining in, I started disagreeing with him, told him that he was full of shit. True, I had flunked out of school in Paris, but, when it came to the French vernacular, my ear could not be faulted. Lowell did not seem to notice my increasing nastiness, but his two groupies certainly did. Finally, I said goodnight and split. I walked from the Upper West Side down to my room in the Village, fuming and muttering like an old drunk.

Another time I was drinking red wine, chain-smoking, and writing, long past midnight. Suddenly, the poem took off, the words just flowing, in my head a merry-go-round of the most brilliant similes and metaphors. This is it! I was convinced there had never been such a moment of inspiration in the whole history of literature. I reread what I'd written and had to quit my desk and walk around the room, I got so excited. No sooner was I finished with one poem than I started another even more incredible one. Toward daybreak, paying no attention to my neighbor's furious banging on the wall, I typed them out with my two fingers and finally passed out exhausted on the bed. In the morning I dragged myself to work, dead tired but happy.

When evening came, I sat down to savor what I wrote the night before, a glass of wine in my hand. The poems were terrible! Incoherent babble, surrealist drivel! How could I have written such crap? I was stunned, depressed, and totally confused.

It wasn't the last time this had happened: nights of creative bliss followed by days of gagging. With great clarity I could see every phony move I had made, every borrowing, every awkwardness. Then I found myself in a different kind of rush: I had only seconds left to rip it up, burn, and flush down the toilet all these poems before the doctors and nurses rushed in and put me in a straitjacket. Of course, the next night I was at it again, writing furiously and shaking my head in disbelief at the gorgeous images and metaphors flooding out of my pen.

I have thrown out hundreds of poems in my life, four chapters of a novel, the first act of a play, fifty or so pages of a book on Joseph Cornell. Writing poetry is a supreme pleasure, and so is wiping the slate clean.

I was five minutes late from lunch at the insurance company where I was working, and my boss chewed me out for being thoughtless in front of twenty or so other drudges. I went and sat at my desk for a while fuming, then I rose slowly, wrapped my scarf around my neck and put my gloves on in plain view of everyone, and walked out without looking back. I didn't have an overcoat, and it was snowing, but I felt giddy, deliriously happy at being free.

Here's a scene for you. My father and I are walking down Madison Avenue when I spot a blue overcoat in a store window. We study it, comment on the cut, and my father suggests I try it on. I know he has no money on him or in the bank, but he insists since it's beginning to snow a little and I'm only wearing a tweed jacket.

We go in, I put it on, and it fits perfectly. Of course, I'm in love with it. We ask the price, and it's two hundred dollars— which was a lot of money in 1961. Too bad, I think, but then my father asks me if I want it. I figure maybe he's showing off in front of a salesman, or he's come into some money he has not told me about. "Do you want it?" he asks again while the salesman discreetly busies himself elsewhere. "You have no money, George," I remind him, expecting him to contradict me or come to his senses. "Don't worry" is his mysterious reply.

I've seen him do this before, and it embarrasses me. He asks to see the boss, and they sequester themselves while I wait around waiting for us to be laughed at and kicked out on our asses. Instead, he emerges triumphant, and I wear the overcoat into the street. He is a con man manqué. His manner and appearance inspired such confidence that with a small down payment and promise to pay a small weekly amount, he'd get what he wanted. This was in the days before credit cards and credit bureaus, when the store owners had to make credit decisions on the spot. They trusted him, and they were right. He paid eventually what he owed them. He pulled this stunt only in the best stores. It would never occur to him to ask for credit from a grocer, and so he often went hungry while remaining impeccably dressed.

My father had phenomenal debts. He borrowed money everywhere and paid his bills only after a second or third notice. It was nothing for him to spend the rent money the night before it was due. I lived in terror of my landlords, while he seemingly never worried. We'd meet after work, and he'd suggest dinner in an Italian restaurant, and I'd resist knowing it was once more his rent money he was proposing to spend. He'd describe the dishes and wines we could be having in tantalizing detail, and I'd keep reminding him of the rent. Then he'd get mad. As if I was feeble-minded, he'd explain to me slowly, painstakingly, that one should never worry about the future. We'll never be so young as we are tonight. If we are smart, and we are, tomorrow we'll figure out how to pay the rent. Bello Giorgio, one waitress in Chicago used to call him. At the age of fifty-three, with his hair thinning and slicked back, he could pass for an Italian or a South American. There was no resisting him. We happily spent the rent money.

On a hot night in a noisy, crowded, smoke-filled jazz club, whiskey and beer were flowing; everyone was reeling with drink. A fat woman laughed so hard, she fell off her chair. It was difficult to hear the music. Someone took a muted trumpet solo I tried to follow with my left ear, while with my right I had to listen to two woman talk about a fellow called Mike who was a scream in his bathing suit.

It was better to go to clubs on weeknights, when the crowd was smaller and there were no tourists. Best of all was walking in after midnight, in time to catch the final set of the night. One night when I arrived, the bass and the drums were already playing, but where was Sonny Rollins, whom I came to hear? Finally, we heard a muffled saxophone: Sonny was in the men's room, blowing his head off. Everybody quieted down, and soon enough he came through the door, bobbing his shaved head, dark shades propped on a nose fit for an emperor. He was playing "Get Happy," twisting it inside out, reconstituting it completely, discovering its concealed rhythmic and melodic beauties, and we were right there with him, panting with happiness.

It was great. The lesson I learned was: cultivate controlled anarchy. I found Rollins, Charlie Parker, and Thelonious Monk far better models of what an artist could be than most poets. The same was true of the painters. Going to jazz clubs and galleries made me realize that there was a lot more poetry in America than one could find in the quarterlies.

I went to see Ionesco's *Bald Soprano* with Uncle Boris one Saturday afternoon in a small theater in the Village. There were only six people in the audience for the matinee, and that included the two of us. They gave the performance anyway. When it came to the love scene with the woman who has three noses, the actors got carried away on the couch. Their voices went down to a whisper as they started undressing each other. Is this in the script? Boris and I looked at each other puzzled. The other four people were suddenly nowhere to be seen. The two on the stage did not fuck each other, but they came pretty close. I must admit I have no recollection of the rest of the play except that the street at the exit was covered with freshly fallen snow.

I met a painter in a bar, an older fellow living in poverty with a wife and two small kids in a cold-water flat, where he painted huge, realistic canvasses of derelicts. A skyscraper and underneath a poor man begging. The message was obvious, but some of the faces were nicely painted.

Despite the difference in our ages, we saw each other quite a bit, talking about art and literature, until one day I showed him my poems. We were sitting in his kitchen with a bottle of whiskey between us. He leaned back in the chair and read the poem slowly as if he had just learned to read. At some point I saw his expression change. He was beginning to look annoyed and even angry. Finally, he looked at me as if seeing me for the first time and said something like: "Simic, I thought you were a smart kid. This is pure shit you're writing."

His bluntness stunned me. I left his place shortly afterward in a daze. I was convinced he was right. If I had a pistol, I would have shot myself on the spot. Then, little by little, mulling over what he said, I got pissed off. There were good things in my poems, I thought. "Fuck him," I shouted at some man who came my way in the street. Of course, the son of a bitch was right, too, and it hurt me that he was, but all the same . . .

I came out of my daze just as I was entering Central Park on Fifty-ninth Street. I had walked more than sixty blocks totally oblivious of my surroundings. I sat on a bench and reread my poems, crossing out most of the lines, attempting to rewrite them then and there, still angry, still miserable, and at the same time grimly determined.

One evening in a restaurant, a nice, old, silver-haired lady, pointing to three other silver-haired ladies smiling at us from the next table, asked Boris and me: "Would you, please, tell us what language you are speaking?"

Boris, who never missed an opportunity to play a joke, made a long face, sighed once or twice, and—with moist eyes and a sob in his voice—informed her that, alas, we were the last two remaining members of a white African tribe speaking a now nearly extinct language.

That surprised the hell out of her! She didn't realize, she told us, now visibly confused, that there were native white African tribes.

"The best-kept secret in the world," Boris whispered to her and nodded solemnly, while she rushed back to tell her friends.

It was part of being an immigrant and living in many worlds at the same time, some of which were imaginary. After what we had been through, the wildest lies seemed plausible. The poems that I was going to write had to take that into account.

19

Always plenty of good food and wine at Uncle Boris's. The four of us at the table take turns uncorking new bottles. We drink out of water glasses the way they do in the old country. "More bread!" somebody yells. There's never enough bread, never enough olives, never enough soup. We are eating through our second helping of thick bean soup after having already polished off a dozen smoked sausages and a couple of loaves of bread.

And we argue with mouths full. My uncle Boris would make Mother Teresa reach for a baseball bat. He likes to make big pronouncements, to make the earth tremble with his political and artistic judgments. You drop your spoon. You can't believe your ears. Suddenly, you are short of breath and choking as if you had swallowed a big fly.

"Is he kidding?" I hear myself say, my voice raising to a falsetto. I am the reasonable type. I try to lay out the pros and cons as if I were a judge making a summation to the jury. I believe in the calming effect of an impeccable logical argument. Before I can get very far, my brother interrupts to tell me that I'm full of shit. His philosophy is: the more reasonable it sounds, the less likely it is that it's true. My father, on the other hand, always takes the Olympian view. "None of you know what the fuck you're talking about," he informs us and resumes slurping his soup.

Before we can all gang up on him, the pork roast is served. The skin is brown and crusty with a bit of fat underneath. There are potatoes and onions in the pan, soaked in the drippings. We are in heaven. The new bottle of wine is even better. Nuit Saint Georges is my father's favorite wine, since his name is George. That's the only one he buys when he is flush.

For a while we don't say anything. We just grunt with our

faces in our plates. My aunt is carving more meat, while my uncle runs into the kitchen to get those hot little red Mexican peppers he forgot all about.

Unfortunately, one of us starts on politics. Immediately, we start arguing again. In the last few years Boris has become very conservative. He loves Barry Goldwater. He loves Nixon. As for Bobby Kennedy, he's a Russian agent, if you ask him. Boris even warned the *New York Times* about that, but they didn't print the letter, of course. Tonight he shouts that I am a Communist, too. He has suspected it for years and had his final proof just two minutes ago.

I have no idea what I said to make him think that, so I ask him to please repeat it. He's appalled. No guts, he says. Feigning innocence, backtracking. Jesus Christ! He calls on the heavens to witness.

"It's what you said about Hoover," my brother says, guffawing. Both he and my father are enjoying themselves, while I'm debating whether to punch Boris in the mouth. He's really pissed, too. He says I even look like Trotsky with my wire-rimmed glasses. "Get me the FBI on the phone," he yells to my aunt. He's going to speak to J. Edgar personally about me.

It's hard to tell with Boris if he's entirely serious. He loves scenes. He loves opera. It's the third act, we are all dead on the stage, and he is caterwauling. Without histrionics life is boring. This is bliss as far as he's concerned.

Watching him rant like that, I get an inspiration. I rise from the table, walk over, and solemnly kiss him on the top of his bald head. He's stunned, speechless! It takes him some time to collect himself. Finally, he smiles sheepishly and embraces me in return.

"Forget about the FBI," he yells to my aunt in the kitchen. She comes out with enough different cheeses to open a store. We eat and drink and converse politely. The old guys are reminiscing about the war.

Is it true one grows nostalgic even about the horrors as one grows old? Probably. I'm nostalgic about an August afternoon after the war. My mother, brother, and I were being escorted at gunpoint and on foot from one prison to the other. At some point we walked past an apple orchard, and our guard let us stop and pick apples. Not a care in the world. Munching the apples and chatting with our guard.

As for my father and Boris, it seems that when they were in Trieste they used to pull this stunt. My father would invite friends to a fancy restaurant, but, when the time came to pay the bill, he'd send Boris to break the news to the unsuspecting owner that they were completely broke.

"You were very good at it," my father assures him.

Boris, when he's not raving, looks like an English gentleman and has the appropriate clothes and fine manner to go along with his face. The owner of the restaurant would accept his apologies and his promise to settle the bill expeditiously and would even permit his financially strapped guests to order another round of brandies before going off into the night.

"It's his smile," we all agree. Boris has the sweetest, shiest smile when he's happy. Old ladies, especially, adore him. Nobody knows how to bow and kiss their hands like he does. It's hard to believe he was once a guard in a maximum-security prison in Australia. Come to think of it, none of us, individually or collectively, makes much sense. We are all composite characters, made up of a half-dozen different people, thanks to being kicked around from country to country.

Boris, for instance, right now is sighing. He studied opera singing for years, tried to make a career of it, and failed. Now he sings only when he's happy. He has a huge, beautiful tenor voice, but no ear. When he starts hitting the high notes, you have to run for your life. It's no use. He can be heard across the street. He has the world's loudest voice, and it's off-key.

He sings for us an aria from *Othello*. We survive that somehow, but he's not through yet. We are going to hear Tristan's death scene. Across the table my father looks grim. My brother has vanished. I am lying on the floor at Tristan's feet trying my best to keep a straight face. Boris paces up and down conducting the Berlin Philharmonic as he sings. From time to time he stops to translate for us. "Tristan is going mad," he whispers. No doubt about that! This Tristan is ready for the loony bin. His tongue is lolling, and his eyes are popping out of his head. He's standing on the sofa and leaning against the wall, arms spread, as if he is about to be crucified.

"Verflucht wer dich gebrant!" he shreiks.

"Stop it, Boris," my aunt says calmly, coming in from the kitchen with the cake.

"Please let him sing the death scene, Auntie," I say, and now even my father has to grin.

You have to admire the man's love of music. Boris confessed to me once that he could never sing in the real opera house. He'd get so excited on the stage, he'd jump into the orchestra pit at the conclusion of his aria.

Now we applaud him. We are thirsty and hungry again, and so is he, luckily. My brother has reappeared.

"I'm going to bed," my aunt announces after she brings back the cheese and cold cuts. She knows this is not going to end soon. We are on our favorite topic, the incredible stupidity of our family.

I don't know if all large families indulge in such orgies of self-abuse, but we made a specialty of it. I don't think it's pretense either. I mean, it's not like we believe secretly that we are really superior and this is just talk. Our family history is a story of endless errors of judgment, of bad situations made even worse by bickering.

"Imagine this," my father says. "There's a war on, the Nazis, the Ustashi, the Hungarians, the Romanians, the Chetniks, the Italians, the Bulgarians, the Communists, are killing us, and even the English and the Americans are dropping bombs. So, what do we do to make things really interesting? We all take different sides in that war so we can really make life miserable for each other."

We are silent with the weight of our drunkenness and the sad truth of my father's last remark. Finally, Boris looks up and says, "How about a really great bottle of wine?"

We all look at Boris, puzzled, but he explains that this wine is supposed to be very special, very old, very expensive.

"What is it?" we want to know.

He's not telling. He's going to decant it in the cellar so we can blind-taste it and guess its origins.

Very well. Off he goes, and he's gone so long we are beginning to think the bastard sneaked off to bed. Instead, he returns with an air of mystery carrying a bottle wrapped in a towel. The last time Boris had a bottle of expensive wine he had us sip it from a teaspoon. He went around the dinner table pouring drops of a fine old Margot onto a spoon and making us all in turn say, "Aaaaaahh," like a baby doctor.

This time we just get clean glasses, and he pours everybody a little taste. It's red wine. There's no doubt about that even at three in the morning. We twirl it around in our glasses, sniff it like real pros, and take a sip. I think it's Chianti, my father says it's a Burgundy, my brother mentions Spanish wine but is not sure.

Boris is triumphant! Here's the final proof! Serbs as a people, and the members of this family especially, are all know-nothings, show-offs, and the world's biggest phonies.

Then, to rub it in, he tells us how he found out recently that the Sicilian who pumps his gas in Brooklyn makes his own wine. "Probably in the same bathtub where he washes his ass," he adds for effect. Anyway, the man gave him a bottle for Christmas, and this is what we are drinking.

It still tastes pretty good, but on second thought, we have to admit, we made complete fools of ourselves. Of course, we can barely keep our eyes open. The day is breaking. For the moment we have run out of talk. We just look at each other, yawning occasionally. The house is quiet. Even the cops are catching forty winks in their patrol car on the corner.

"How about some ice cream?" Boris asks.

My great-grandfather, Philip
Simic, in 1890s

My father at age of three

My grandfather in 1918

My grandfather and father
in 1921

My father with a suckling pig,
New Year's 1928

My mother in 1933

My father with unknown
friends in 1934

Father with Gypsies at the Red
Rooster Tavern, 1935

Mother and father on
the terrace of our
apartment, 1938

With mother on the streets of
Belgrade in 1940

Winter 1941(?) with mother

Uncle Boris singing in a nightclub in 1944

In the village of my maternal grandfather in 1940(?)

Father and I, returning from a soccer game in 1942(?)

Father in Elizabeth City, North
Carolina, 1952

Yugoslav passport issued
18 June 1953

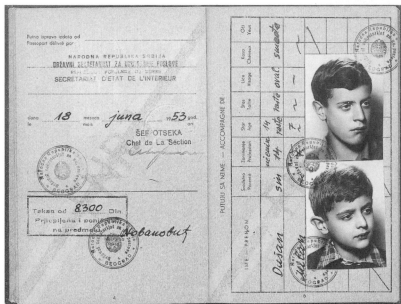

In Paris on Avenue des Champs Elysées in 1953

Ready for the night on the town, Paris 1954

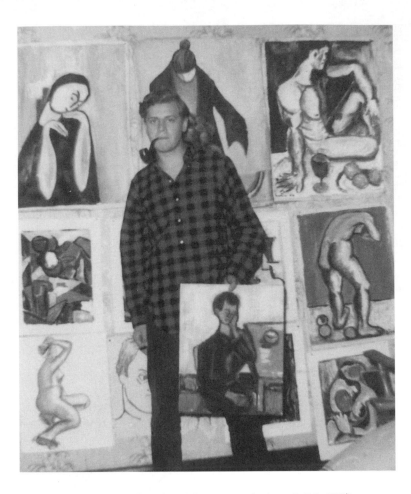

In Oak Park, Illinois, with some paintings I did, 1957

On lunch hour, New York,
April 1960

As a military policeman in
Toul, France, 1963

Back from the Army, New York, 1963

20

There was an old fellow in Washington Square Park who used to lecture me about Sacco and Vanzetti and the great injustice done to them. We'd share a bench from time to time, and I'd hear him say again and again how if shit were worth money the poor people would be born without assholes. He wore gray gloves, walked with a cane, tipped his hat to the ladies, and worried about me. "A kid just off the boat," he'd say to someone passing by. "Sure to get screwed if he doesn't watch out."

We all secretly think we are pretty smart. Beneath our air of modesty, we are as smug as eighteenth-century aristocrats are. I was no different. I went around with my nose in the air convinced I had a pretty cozy setup: a place to live, a job, and few friends. I was even writing poetry daily, enriching the U.S. Post Office with my submissions to literary magazines. Every lunch hour I dashed home to check the mail, dispose of the rejection slips, and instantly readdress the poems to some other publication. At the age of twenty-three it is not unreasonable to be optimistic.

On one of these lunch hour visits I ran into a burglar inside my apartment. I carried a bag of groceries in one hand, the mail in the other, and was making my way down a long, dark corridor toward the kitchen when I collided with a strange man. He was small, my age, and as surprised to see me as I was to see him. He shouldn't be here, my brain told me after what was an eternity. I dropped the bag I was carrying and grabbed the man, who was still standing before me, by the nose, when he pulled away and run into the kitchen. He wants to get a knife, I thought, so I rushed back into the living room and picked up a chair. Nothing happened. I could hear the traffic on the street, my own heart beating, but not much else. "I'm going to kill you, you son of a bitch," I yelled out once and then twice more. "Motherfucker, piece of shit, I'm coming," I roared, and I did, advancing very carefully with the chair raised over my head. Of course, I was terrified but had no choice. It was a matter of honor, territorial prerogative, so to speak. Finally, I turned the corner and stepped into the kitchen. The back door was open; there was no one there. I put down the chair I was carrying and sat down. I could have been knifed, left bleeding on the floor. Since I lived alone it would have taken a long time for someone to find me.

After that day, coming home and unlocking the door always produced an anxious moment or two. Especially late at night. One night I stuck my head in, hesitated with the door still open, and heard the mousetrap snap in the dark. Indeed, when I turned the lights on, there was a mouse in it wriggling to free his broken leg.

Talk about surprises, another time I came home during the lunch hour to find a draft notice. I knew vaguely there was a possibility, since I only attended school at night and had no proper deferment, but it never occurred to me this would actually happen. This was 1961. No one I knew was being drafted—and here it was, in black-and-white on Department of the Army stationery, with my name and address, the order that I present myself at 0600 hours on September 25 at 30 Whitehall Street, and no song and dance. It took minutes, hours, days, for the contents of the letter to sink in.

It was Friday, I remember. I had less than a month of freedom left. I called the office, told them what happened, and said I was taking the afternoon off. Ordinarily, this being the busiest day of the week at the payroll office, Angelo and Virginia would have given me hell. I had a way with all the squawkers who didn't get their overtime paid that week or had some other complaint. My strategy was to agree with the hotheads 100 percent even when they were 100 percent wrong. I took their side and raged myself about their incompetent supervisors who are always trying to screw hardworking guys like them. After such an outburst on my part, they lost sight of the probability that the payroll office may be the culprit. They went away befuddled, while a new belligerent barged in waving his pay envelope.

In the meantime, I was in a bar across the street from my apartment having a shot of whiskey. Next, I remember walking without purpose on the crowded Fifth Avenue, sitting on the steps of the Public Library, eating a hamburger for dinner on Eighth Street and staring into space and waking at daybreak and noticing the draft notice on the floor next to my shoes. It always said the same thing: no reprieve from inexorable fate.

The worse thing about such a stroke of bad luck is that one has to listen to people's commiserations. I'd blurt my news, show my letter, and sit there listening to the condolences and advice. With the best of intentions people tried to cheer me up: I'll see the world and have all kinds of interesting experiences. I'll have the right to the GI Bill afterward, I'll look good in a uniform, etc.

The weather that September, as it always is in New York, was glorious. Blue skies, dry, warm days and cool nights ideal for long strolls. I noticed things I had not noticed before. Buildings in my neighborhood, stores, faces of people going about their daily errands. How strange the cities are with their sand-grain manyness. Ordinarily, so much of it is invisible to us, until a day comes when each face strikes suddenly with its luminous singularity. That strange, simultaneous sense of their permanence and their mortality. I'll be gone, and they'll be still here pouring out of the subway entrance. It is the simplest truths that are most astonishing. I stood watching them and couldn't get enough.

How quickly the days go by when you don't want them to go by quickly. I was torn: I craved solitude, and I craved company, which meant I always wanted to be someplace else. The trouble was that I had hundreds of practical matters to attend to. Everything I owned I suddenly had no use for. The saying "You can't take it away with you" applied here too. I gave books, records, pots and pans, to everybody I knew, and there was still more junk to dispose of. I could not even take my poems along. I put them all in a shoebox and gave them to my father.

If not for the endless worries, there would not be much else inside our heads. Every one of us is a brainchild of Old Man Trouble. I never got enough sleep in my life. I've lain in the dark for sixty years sweating over everything from my own life to the world's vileness and stupidity. The metaphysician at 3 A.M., that's me. I'd put on a brave face in the morning, go to work, and do what I was supposed to do with a cheerful face. Back then, friends took me to festive lunches and dinners. Young women who ordinarily paid me no attention kissed me on the cheek and stroked my head. I was "poor Charlie" all day long. Off into the unknown, where new hassles await him. My misfortune suddenly made me attractive.

The day was fast approaching. The weather continued to be balmy. Everyone else seemed not to have a care in the world. They made plans for parties and trips in my presence, lucky bastards. I said less and less, just nodded to everything anyone said. In my mind I was already elsewhere—or more accurately nowhere, since I had no idea what to expect. When the day finally came, I was glad. It was like being strapped in the electric chair and suddenly growing curious how the contraption works. My hand trembled a little while I shaved. On my way to the subway I saw only a drunk sleeping in a doorway. I remember nothing of the ride downtown. Outside the induction center there was a small crowd gathered. No one said much of anything. We filed in when the door opened, and that was that. I was too tired to have any kind of thoughts. I just did what I was told and resigned myself to whatever came next.

It was pitch-dark when we got off the buses. It took a while to sort out all the recruits, break them into platoons, and march them off into the barracks. The buses drove off into the night, and a dozen of us remained with a sergeant in the parking lot. The moon was out, a nice cool night, pleasant for sleeping. Instead, the sergeant made us "police" the area. In the lingo of the army *policing* means picking up trash, cigarette butts, and what have you. That was explained to us, but not how to do it in the dark. In fact, someone complained that it was hard to see anything, only to be shouted at and called names. I said nothing. I just went around bent over like Groucho Marx, squinting at the ground and mistaking small pebbles for butts, finding nothing but continuing to search the area diligently.

It's amazing how quickly one turns into an obedient drudge in an army or a big company. It took me no time to realize that I was now a dog whose master carried a big stick. The ones who did not got in all kinds of trouble. It frightened me how quickly I lost whatever little self-respect I had. I spoke only when spoken to by my superiors and then only to say yes. During all my waking hours I strove to achieve complete anonymity and would have succeeded but for the wire-rimmed glasses I wore. "Are you a preacher, son?" an old sergeant asked me once. In the line at the mess hall, the day after we were assigned to a training company, a black sergeant stopped and asked every one of us individually what we did in civilian life. When I replied, "Payroll clerk," he spat on the ground and said, "Shit." He said the same thing to everyone else, being especially sneering of college students. Only when the fellow in front of me said he was a musician did he break into a smile. What kind? he wanted to know. I play jazz trumpet, the recruit replied. The sergeant wanted to know more. He was polite, genuinely interested, friendly. There's no justice in this world, we all thought.

I'm a shithead, is how the soldier at the entrance to our company area greeted everyone who came by. He'd remove his helmet, bow, and say what he was told to say by some NCO. I forget what he did to deserve that, but he remained at his post one whole day and late into the night. The main intent of basic training is to terrify the recruit into submission. No matter what we did or did not do, we were yelled at, told a hundred times every day that we were the dumbest sons of bitches ever to serve in the army. The sergeants competed with each other in finding new ways to belittle us. I was a drooling, sorry-ass fuck-off and thousands of other things. After eight weeks of being cussed at and called names, I was a doormat. I took it and didn't bat an eyelash. I stared them straight in the face. A bunch of nobodies, field manure for the next war led by a bunch of windbags who call themselves officers.

It's good to have things clear like that. Mutual hatred and fear, and that included the other recruits. Sure, there were a few I got along with fabulously, but the rest were the kind of people you ordinarily would not want to spend two minutes with. In civilian life we have the luxury of fussily choosing our companions. Not here. The world's most boring human being is now your bunkmate, telling his life story every night. Tired as I was, I had no difficulty falling asleep, but he'd reach down from the upper bunk and shake me awake to hear the rest. "Familiarity breeds contempt," my friend Virginia always gave us an explanation for not tying herself to any man. There's camaraderie in the small outfits, but in basic training, with its rounds of discipline, punishment, and humiliations, it's hard to have more than one or two casual friends.

Rainy night in November in New Jersey. We are bivouacking in the woods, sleeping under tents, and I'm on guard duty long after midnight, pacing up and down a stretch of dirt road, getting soaked despite the poncho and helmet I'm wearing. All of a sudden, I see a white blur in the woods coming in my direction. It's a soldier in his long johns hopping like a rabbit. I'm astonished but remember to point my rifle and ask for a password as I was ordered to do. He has no clue what I'm talking about. I'm supposed to arrest him, call the guard post, and have him picked up; instead, I ask him what the hell is he doing here dressed like that. It seems he crawled out of his pup tent to take a piss, walked some distance to insure the pee wouldn't trickle back to where he was sleeping, and promptly got lost himself. Now he can't find his way back. It's pouring and pitch-dark, and I only have the vaguest notion where I am myself. Can't help you, is all I can say. After standing there for a while, he's off again, hopping back into the woods. I never saw him again. Did he find his tent? Probably not. He could be still there thirty-five years later, white-haired and white-bearded, still looking for his tent.

After six weeks in the army it was hard to believe that I had any previous life. The thought that there was a time when I, myself, made the decision when to go to sleep and when to wake up seemed improbable. I still remember vividly the sight of Manhattan across the Jersey marshes on my first pass after six weeks in Fort Dix. It was about eight in the evening, a chilly but clear November night. It looked unreal. The eerinesss persisted while I walked the streets of the city. The buildings were phantasms and the people walking around ghosts. Even when I was ordering my dinner in an Italian restaurant in the Village that I knew well, a part of me did not believe any of it was really there.

That feeling of unreality wore off after a day, but it would reoccur, sometimes with no apparent cause.

I have no idea why the army picked me to be a military policeman. They did the same with my brother a few years later, so it must be some psychological trait the battery of tests we were given brought to light. It was bizarre. I always hated cops and professors, and I ended up being both in my life. Whatever the true reason, I spent the winter of 1961–62 in Fort Gordon, Georgia, learning about law enforcement and military justice. That was all very nice, but what really interested me and everybody else is, what happens next? The most likely outcome, the one we all feared, was that I'll end up in Korea patrolling the edge of the demilitarized zone while being sniped at by the Commies. The other crummy possibility was some small army base in the Deep South or in Texas. To my great astonishment the army sent me to Kaislerslatern, Germany, to guard a depot supposedly full of secret weapons.

We crossed the Atlantic on a World War II troop ship in bad weather. My job was to clean latrines, always an awful prospect, made even more odious by the fact that most of the four thousand soldiers on board were seasick. For some reason I, myself, was not, although many times I came close to throwing up. With everybody sick and in their bunks, I had the ship almost to myself. We were not allowed on the deck because of the weather, but a couple of times I snuck out behind the sailors. It was windy, cold: the sea and the sky, gray and stormy. Very invigorating and also very scary. Nature lovers, romantics—there was nothing for them here. Rather, one thought of the old sailors, fishermen going after the cod into the unknown in their little boats long before America was discovered. Even this old tub didn't seem too trustworthy. The ship screeched, squealed, made awful grinding noises, rattled, seemed to be coming apart. It was especially bad at night. The waves were like huge fists banging somewhere above. In between them, in the brief respite, there was the sound of someone vomiting to keep me awake. In short, a round-the-clock horror movie.

We disembarked in Bremenhaven, and they put some of us on the night train south. I stayed up staring into the dark.

Occasionally, there was a poorly lit city, a quick view of some long street or apartment house that reminded me of Belgrade and films about World War II. The sight of a few Germans and the sound of the language, whenever we stopped, were also disconcerting. Here was the bad dream I thought I had escaped. It was just like I never left.

I stayed only three months in K-town, as the GIs used to call it, before being transferred to France. I asked for it, wrote a letter pointing out the many ways in which my knowledge of French will benefit the army. Of course, I expected nothing to happen, but one morning the company commander called me into his office and gave me the new orders. In Toul I was going to be a regular cop, patrol the local towns in a jeep or a squad car, and take drunken GIs back to the post and throw them in jail. When I arrived, it turned out, they had different plans for me. They made me a liaison to the French police in Nancy. It meant I wore civvies, sat in an office in police headquarters, took my coffee in cafés, lunches in small restaurants in the neighborhood, read French newspapers for hours while sitting at my desk. In the four months that I worked there, I can only recollect a few instances where I actually had to do some translating.

Once I was in a French court and had the painful duty of telling a GI who had run over some kid that he was going to jail. He guessed as much from the judge's stern demeanor but nevertheless turned to me hopefully. If I had been alone, I would have stalled, but there, in an almost full courtroom, there was no choice except to tell him straight.

Another time I found myself translating for an air force general who was meeting his French counterpart. We were taken for a tour of some radar equipment, and their talks got so technical I had no idea (in any language) what the hell it all meant. I could see they were annoyed with me, on the verge of asking, Who sent this phony? Luckily, the two of them repaired to the service club for a drink, and after a few rounds the subjects of their conversation changed from military matters to women. All of a sudden I was translating at top speed, making the two tough old birds laugh, to the displeasure of the junior officers, who stood across the room watching us party. It ended up, after many more toasts, with the two generals proclaiming loudly that I was the best translator they ever had. I thought for sure, my job is safe, I'll spend the rest of my tour lazing in cafés, smoking Gitanes, and watching women.

Unfortunately, the word got back to my outfit about the cushy life I was leading. I was placed on regular duty, which meant mostly breaking bar fights, covering motor vehicle accidents, and otherwise driving around for hours on the streets of Toul and Nancy. Then, one day, they demoted me even farther. I received a temporary transfer to a tiny military police unit at a base some fifty miles away, near the town of Luneville. I began keeping a journal and even attempted a few poems that I discarded long ago. The journal entries were more interesting.

21

We just sit around in our underwear listening to the radio and playing cards. There are four of us. The sergeant has a room of his own on the other side of the kitchen. Now that the weather has turned bad, there is not much police duty. The bus for Luneville leaves at six every evening, but there's hardly anybody on it. Our schedule is very simple. Two of us work every night and don't go patrolling before ten. The patrol drives to Luneville, has a drink at the train station café, checks a few bars frequented by GI's, makes sure everybody is on the 11:30 bus, and concludes the evening with a couple more drinks at the station. On Saturday nights there are a few more soldiers in the bars since the curfew is not till one, but so far there have not been any serious incidents. The police radio is silent. The only time we use it is to ask the patrol on duty to bring back some sandwiches from the train station. We no longer eat in the mess hall. The last time was at Thanksgiving. We all dressed nice in our civvies and strolled over there. We got nothing but dirty looks. Besides, the baked potatoes and the turkey were raw. We never went back. We buy food in St. Clement or eat in its only café. Even the redneck Edward is beginning to discriminate between different kinds of pâté.

The weather in eastern France is awful. In the summer it rains all the time, and in winter it snows when it's not raining. In the month that I've been here, we haven't had a single clear day. It would be very depressing except for the life we are leading. At Toul there were morning formations, alerts, extra duty, and inspections. Here we don't even hang our clothes in our lockers. We just throw everything on the floor. Sgt. Briggs doesn't give a shit. He's in love with a waitress in Luneville and dreams of taking her back to South Dakota. When they have a fight, which is often, I write letters of apology for him in terrible French. It seems she doesn't speak any English and has two little kids. That's all we know.

He's gone a lot during the day. Since there are five of us including the sergeant, we divide our working time this way: two on duty, two on standby, and one off over a twenty-four-hour period. What this means is that nobody works very hard. "We got it made," PFC Williams keeps reminding us. This is what life ought to be, according to him. When he gets back to LA, he's going to open a high-class whorehouse. Then he'll really have it made, he tells us. We think he's kidding about the whorehouse, but he's not. "The best Mexican pussy north of the border at popular American prices." Anytime we are in California we can get it free. We go to bed every night thinking of that.

Edwards caught a wild baby boar on the runway this morning. We were watching the snow falling when we noticed a huge boar strolling on the runway with four little ones behind. The moment he saw it, Edwards took off. We thought he was out of his mind. Surely the mother boar would turn on him, and he'd be in big trouble. She didn't. She was running, and he was running, and the four sucklings were trying to keep up with the mother. We saw him dive and grab one. The mother didn't even look back.

Mace and I think we should eat him. Sgt. Briggs thinks it might not be a good idea. Like, it's French property, and there's some kind of Army regulation about eating French property. In the meantime, the piglet—or what ever you call it—is very frightened. It won't eat anything we offer it, and Edwards wants to keep it as a pet.

There are no planes on the runway. None ever land. The runway is there in case of war. If the Russians cross the East German border, they'll be here in three days. Our woods are full of concealed trucks, jeeps, and armored vehicles, which three hundred or so soldiers keep in constant readiness. That is, they change the oil, check air pressure in the tires, and occasionally take them for a spin. The rest of the time they sit around dying of boredom, or they raise hell in Luneville or in their service club.

This "club," by the way, is just a shack with a few tables, chairs, and a jukebox. We don't go near the place unless we have to. We throw the drunks into our cells to sleep it off and in the morning send them back to their units.

We also have forty Poles under our jurisdiction. They pull guard duty around the post. They are what's left of the heroic General Anders's army, which fought alongside the Allies in the Italian campaign. These are people who couldn't emigrate or find some civilian employment. They are mostly in their fifties, and they're all drunks. The post commander at times complains to Sgt. Briggs that he finds one of them asleep at the front gate, but no one does anything about it.

We had a debate this morning whether to give the piglet to the Poles or to our maintenance man, François. He was supposed to be coming to fix the toilet, and he's an enterprising, friendly sort of guy. We were still undecided when he showed up. The piglet was in the corner of the kitchen, looking sickly. It hadn't eaten anything in three days. "You want him?" Briggs said. Before the rest of us could react, François had the pig tied and thrown into his truck. Of course, we were invited to the roast. I knew none of us would go. We had looked too long into the eyes of that pig.

Tonight Briggs and I drove as far as St. Dié. It's a strange, modern-looking town, apparently completely rebuilt after burning down during the war. At the restaurant where we stopped to eat, they were surprised to see American soldiers. There are none in the area. They were friendly, and the food was superb. After the second bottle of wine, it was hard to leave. Outside it was cold and snowing a little. "Not as bad as in South Dakota," Briggs said. He is a poor country boy. He loves the army. He loves France, or, more precisely, he loves a French waitress. He loves South Dakota too. As for me, I love wine and bean soup and sausages and good country bread.

On the way back we had a slight worry that there might be an emergency. For several miles the mountains prevented us from getting clear radio reception, but the static told us something was going on. Suppose there was a serious car accident or a fight in a bar, and they couldn't get in touch with us. There'd be hell to pay. It turned out to be just Mace asking for sandwiches and beer.

Today (Saturday) we had plenty to do for a change. At four in the afternoon we were playing cards, still not fully dressed, when the phone rang. There had been a knifing in the service club. Sgt. Briggs and I went in one jeep and Mace and Williams in the other. Edwards stayed by the radio. We got there so fast people were still running away from the club. Inside we almost stumbled on a man lying on the floor with a knife sticking out of his chest. Well, that took my breath away. Holy shit! This was serious business. The bartender pointed in the direction the culprits had gone. Briggs and I took out after them on foot, while Mace called the medics.

Briggs was running ahead through the woods, and I was trying to keep after him, when we spotted a couple of guys ahead. One was running deeper into the woods, and the other was turning toward the open fields. Briggs yelled at me to take that one.

Here we were, then, racing across the fields, with me out of breath calling on him to stop and falling behind, when I pulled out my pistol and fired once into the air. I didn't even think about it. I just wasn't going to run anymore. My man stopped instantly! He even fell to his knees with his back turned to me and waited for me to approach him. "I know my rights," he kept jabbering as I led him back to the club.

Briggs had gotten his pal. They were a couple of country boys whose life was made miserable by a mean sergeant. Today they could take it no more. By the time we brought them back to the station, they were in a party mood. They were laughing about it. "Did you see his face when that knife went in?" one of them kept saying to the other. Mace, a tough black dude from Detroit, was appalled by their hilarity. They were drunk, of course, and the man they stabbed wasn't dead. Still, in all, that night Mace took me aside and warned me about rednecks. "They're all sick in the head," he said. He included Briggs and Edwards. He had a theory about it. "It's all that sheep fucking," he assured me.

I know something about that. One night in Toul, French cops came to our police station and, after much beating around the bush, finally blurted out that they had caught an American

soldier fucking a farmer's sheep. When I got back to the bar-
racks and reported to the card players what had happened,
they all pretended astonishment at my astonishment. Didn't we
fuck animals in the city?

Not many towns look good in the dead of winter, and Luneville
is no exception. Its claim to fame is the once-elegant chateau
where a certain Duchess Elizabeth-Charlotte had fashioned a
famous court that competed with Versaille in its splendor. Vol-
taire was supposed to have been a frequent visitor. Perhaps he
walked the gray streets of Luneville just as I'm doing now, imag-
ining the life of Candide.

I find the place depressing. All this gray reminds me of
prison. A town of family penitentiaries. Empty ones, perhaps?
You walk its streets without meeting anyone. You enter a store,
a dark one to be sure, and you wait forever before someone
shuffles out from the back to serve you. In the bookstore I'm the
only customer. In the restaurant too.

It gets better in the afternoon after the school lets out. There
are even grown-ups to be seen shopping for food and having a
drink. That goes on till about seven, when they all vanish. The
streets are uncommonly dark, since all the houses have their
shutters closed. Eight o'clock in the evening, and I'm the only
one left, crossing large square and wondering what happened
to all the beautiful girls I saw earlier in the afternoon. Are they
all undressed and in bed? Or are they gorging themselves in the
dark at the family dinner table?

I say "in the dark" because I get the impression that these
people don't want their neighbors to know what they're eating.
They shop for charcuteries in the manner of spies picking up a
roll of film at a secret drop. In the silence of wintry Luneville, I
believe I hear them buttering their bread, slurping their evening
soup, and cutting the meat they like underdone, almost bloody.

The weather is foul, of course. It's damp and raw, and it snows a
little. Then it sleets, making the roads treacherous. Last night
we were returning from "Moon Town" when an MG with army
license plates passed us at a high speed on the curvy, tree-lined
road. A drunken second lieutenant from our base, we figured.

A few miles ahead on the empty road we saw his taillights at an odd angle. He had hit a tree head on. We heard his screams from inside the car, the front end of which was completely smashed. We tried to call the medics on the radio, but there was no contact. "I've got to get to the top of that hill," said Briggs and drove off leaving me with the screaming man.

Just then the last bus from Luneville came along full of drunken soldiers. It stopped, and the passengers stumbled out to take a look. The officer was still screaming, and the drunks wanted to pull him out of the wreck, but I wouldn't let them. We have to wait for the medics, that's the rule, I tried to explain.

Hell no! They were going to save the poor man right then and there, and I could go fuck myself.

This was big trouble. A mean-looking crowd debating whether to lynch me or help that man. I was terrified, and yet I couldn't let them do it. Again, I had to pull my gun out. Jesus Christ, they couldn't believe their eyes! A real bastard! Letting a man suffer like that. They were just getting up the courage to charge me when Briggs and the medics showed up.

After much shouting back and forth, we sent the bus on its way, and the two medics pulled the officer out of the wreck. When they got a better look at his bloody face, the one who seemed to be in charge passed out.

What a mess! There we were in the middle of the night on an empty road with a dying man and a passed-out medic, and his sidekick was so frightened all he could do was wring his hands and shake his head.

Luckily for us, back at the base, Mace had had the sense to alert the French cops, who soon arrived with an ambulance from Luneville. We had only an infirmary on the base, so he had to be taken to a French hospital. That's what the cops did, and we followed them.

At the hospital they put the young officer on the table, and somebody went to wake the doctor on duty. His legs looked badly broken, and his face had lacerations, but there were no other wounds anywhere on him. The only problem was he was vomiting blood. "Internal injuries," said the sleepy young woman who was the doctor. They didn't want to open him here to see what was what and suggested we go to Nancy, at least twenty miles away. We decided to call the American hospital in Metz and ask them what to do. Of course, we got some idiot colonel on the line shouting that French hospitals stink; he wanted us to wait there till daybreak, when he would send a helicopter. We asked the woman doctor her opinion. She shrugged her shoulders, and we understood we better get our fellow to Nancy tout de suite.

Off we went to Nancy, this time in a French ambulance. The roads were icy, but the driver was not holding back. "He's going to kill us all," I thought.

They were monitoring the officer's blood pressure, and it was falling dangerously. I could see it for myself. They had to give him several shots on the way. He moaned, and we looked at each other without saying anything.

In Nancy at the big hospital, it was the same scene. They laid him on the emergency room table and stripped him naked. The elderly doctor who showed up didn't give us much confidence at first; he looked like an old drunk, unshaven, disheveled, and with a butt in the corner of his mouth. His hands, however, were beautiful. He passed them over the dying man's abdomen, touching him everywhere and almost caressing him. He was in no hurry, and he kept puffing on his butt. Finally, he told us that there was no need to open him up. "He's going to be alright," he said. We were incredulous, worried the guy would die and we would end up being court-martialed for disobeying that colonel in Metz, but the doctor was adamant. Plus, his hands made us trust him. They were mesmerizing: the hands of a great musician or a thousand-dollar-a-night whore.

The officer is doing fine, we heard this afternoon. I'm still exhausted from the lack of sleep and the excitement. I'm surprised how quickly we acted. We could have waited for that helicopter, although knowing how things work around here with army, air force, and the French authorities, I doubt that it would've been there at daybreak. I have to hand it to Briggs. Most of the time he looks like a dopey hick, but last night he was lucidity itself. Him and that doc with his wise hands.

We were getting ready for the Poles' Christmas party. Briggs and I were in uniform since we were on duty, and Mace and Williams were in civvies. Edwards volunteered to stay by the radio since he doesn't drink. He loves Pepsi-cola, but you can only get Coke here. He's been miserable about that. His girlfriend in South Carolina sent him a gift package with two bottles of Pepsi. One of them fizzled out crossing the Atlantic, so he ended up with only one. He was going to drink it on Christmas day, but this morning he discovered it was missing from his locker. Mace had hidden it. We watched Edwards search for it, even under his pillow and mattress. Finally, he came over to us, looking very pissed, and said: "Hey guys, where's my Pepsi?"

We told him he was nuts. We didn't know what the fuck he was talking about! And besides, we didn't give a shit about his Pepsi. Then we went back to what we were doing.

Poor Edwards sat on his bunk ready to cry. He sat and sat and wouldn't even have breakfast, he was so crushed. We had to slip out to the toilet to have a good laugh. In the end, when we gave him back the bottle, he managed a teeny smile, but it vanished the moment Mace asked him if he'd give us all a sip on Christmas day. Ha-ha-ha! We told him we were just kidding, and he was happy again.

The Poles' Christmas party was outrageous. Being a Slav myself, I was seated next to the captain, who kept feeding me choice morsels. They had all kinds of smoked fish, pâté, sausages, breads, pickled things, plus cases and cases of champagne and vodka. There were about thirty of us at the long table, and everyone had a bottle of each in front of him and two large glasses, which had to be refilled after each toast. Standing on our feet, we toasted the many beauties of Poland and its women. We gulped the vodka and sipped the champagne. I was drunk after ten minutes, and so was everybody else. The pace was suicidal. The idea, obviously, was to go out of your mind as soon as possible. I've never seen anything like it. Briggs and I had to lower the flag in front of the headquarters at dusk, and dusk came right after lunch. We could hardly stand. As we were folding the flag in the prescribed military manner, we dropped it in the mud. Stars and stripes in the mud! Drunk on duty! They court-martialed for less than that.

Luckily, no one saw us. We managed to pick it up and brush

off the mud somehow. Then we went to bed. We never bothered to patrol that evening.

I went to spend three days in Strasbourg but ended up in Paris. This is how it happened. I had the time off and thought, why not go see the famous cathedral and eat all that good Alsatian food! So I did. I took the train, arrived a Strasbourg in the early afternoon, found a hotel just across from the train station, and went to see the cathedral. It was magnificent. Still, if Gothic art is not your thing, and you hate the Church as an institution, the effect is purely aesthetic.

Then I walked the streets until time for dinner. The weather was dreary, with light snow falling and the women so bundled up you couldn't see what they looked like. I had an enormous meal of *choucroute* and a couple bottles of the finest Riesling, and then I went to the movies and saw *Black Orpheus*. I had already seen it twice before in New York, but there was nothing else showing that looked interesting.

The movie ended a little before eleven, and I went straight to my hotel, undressed, jumped into bed, and turned off the lights. Just before I fell asleep, I suddenly asked myself: What in the world am I going to do in Strasbourg for two more days? Then I remembered there was a train for Paris in ten minutes. All of a sudden I was wide awake. It took me five minutes to dress again, stun the night clerk by checking out in a hurry, and run across the empty square to the station.

There were not many people about. I bought a sleeping coach ticket, and by the time I reached the platform the train was pulling in with all its compartments darkened and its roof covered with snow. Truly a midnight train. I was ushered to my compartment, where my bed was already made. It was like a dream: half of me was still in that hotel bed snug under the down covers, and the other half was here undressing again. No one in the world knows where I am right now, it occurred to me. Not even my fate. I had walked out of my life like those people you read about in the newspapers who disappear without a trace after saying they're just going to the corner to buy a pack of cigarettes. I lay for hours in complete bliss. Why not take another train from Paris to Madrid? I had this enormous sense of freedom and well-being, and then I was sweetly tired, and the train never seemed to stop.

There's not much to do in Paris at six in the morning except sit in a chilly café sipping coffee and reading the papers. Since it was too early to call the friends with whom I usually stayed, I walked from Gare de L'Est to the Grand Boulevards. The morning was cold, so I had to keep a brisk pace. At some point I began to crave bacon and eggs. I'd never seen anyone eat such foods in a French café, but at the next one I asked the waiter if it was possible. He looked at me as though I were a lunatic. I ate four brioche just to appease him.

In the side streets off Boulevard Bonne Nouvelle, there were open bistros where workers were standing at the counter having a glass of red wine. After some hesitation, I went into one and ordered a glass with everybody watching. They could tell I was a foreigner but were not sure what kind. I wasn't the type to be drinking red wine at seven in the morning. After a couple of glasses, I felt wonderful. Again, there was this sense of freedom and adventure. I will do everything differently today, I swore to myself. I'll do things I never had the courage to do, like take a taxi to Rue St. Denis and pick up a whore. In the meantime, the sidewalks were getting busier. There were people to watch. I was having my third glass of red wine and had no intention of moving.

It's always the same. The last evening that I was in Paris there was a terrific party somewhere, and the last train to Luneville left at 12:15. If I wasn't on that train and back at the post by 6:00 A.M. I was officially AWOL. My outfit would cover for me for a while, but something might happen in my absence to bring officers from our headquarters in Toul.

So I spent the evening looking at my watch. The time seemed to fly. At eleven o'clock I was talking to a beautiful girl who was interested in me. She had all the time in the world, while I was debating whether or not to miss the train. But I never do. I slipped out at the very last minute. I was the one running down the empty platform letting the conductor help me jump on the moving train.

This time I traveled second-class, in a compartment full of snoring French soldiers who reeked of wine. I tried to sleep, too, but kept thinking about the party and the girl. I should have stayed, I thought. Once I did go AWOL to Paris—not because of a girl but because of a concert of black gospel music. That was when I was stationed in Toul. I went to pick up my pass on Saturday afternoon only to discover that it had been pulled. My bed wasn't made right during that morning's inspection, and I was being punished. I decided to go anyway. To hell with them. I had a reasonable expectation no one would be looking for me, and my buddies at the entrance gate would not be asking any questions. It was a terrific evening. But I was very worried when I returned on the midnight train and did not sleep a wink. This whole trip I was awake with lovesickness and worried I would sleep through my stop.

As it turned out, I almost froze to death. I got off the local in St. Clement, having changed from the express in Luneville, and started walking to the base. It's about three or four miles up a hill, and the weather was bitter cold, the wind like a whip. I had only a raincoat on, with a sport jacket underneath but no sweater. On my feet I had a pair of light Italian shoes. After a while, my feet started to go numb. It was like walking on air. "Walk faster," I told myself. The higher I got the more cutting the wind was. I could feel each rib, each bone in my body. And then I couldn't. One part of me wanted to sit down and rest, and the other realized the danger. Then I saw the gates of our post and the Polish guard, who walked out to see who was coming on foot so early. What he saw made him run back into the guardhouse for his thermos. Wise Pole, he had vodka in it. I took a big gulp and then another right there in the road. He led me by the hand into his warm shack, where I continued drinking. The old man was delighted to be of service and kept urging me to drink more. I didn't even get drunk. Finally, I walked the rest of the way, found everyone asleep in our station, and went to bed myself.

We were summoned to the main barracks this afternoon, which was strange. They hardly ever call us, even at night when everyone's drunk and getting into fights. They break them up themselves, and that's just fine with us. I've seen MP's in Toul get badly beaten in such situations. You have to have a lot of experience and luck to get out unharmed. "Act quickly," an old sergeant once told me. "Pluck the offender and beat it. Don't stand around arguing military regulations with the drunks."

But this was different. When Mace and Edwards arrived, only a couple of sergeants and an officer were waiting, looking embarrassed. They brought out a short, shy-looking black guy and asked that he be taken into custody. It seems—and this took a while to get straight—he was caught sucking the dick of a corporal who was taking a nap after lunch. A fishy story. Like, supposedly, the corporal's dick had fallen out of his underwear, and he never woke up while the accused was giving him a blow job. They wanted the man out of there while they made arrangements to ship him back to his unit in Germany. Afraid of a lynch mob and the rest.

Mace told us all this while we sat in our station drinking coffee and studying the accused, who stood before us looking miserable.

"Is that true, Willie?" Briggs hollered at him, but poor Willie just hung his head and said nothing.

Willie has been with us four days, and we are used to him. Last night, when Briggs and I came back from patrol, he was playing poker with Mace, Williams, and Edwards.

"The cocksucker's taking all our money," Williams told us, and even Willie had to smile.

Williams wants to take Willie to a whorehouse and straighten him out. He makes him sit for hours at the desk and go through his collection of Scandinavian girlie magazines in preparation. From time to time he checks on him. "How do you like that, Willie?" he says, pointing to some hairy crotch while studying the reaction in Willie's eyes.

Willie is a scrawny, sensitive-looking New York boy. He has a flute, which he plays beautifully when we leave him alone. "Is that Bach?" I asked him one time, and he nodded gravely.

Briggs makes him work. He sweeps, washes the dishes, and scrubs the bathroom. Our place never looked better. We are going to miss him when they take him away.

We keep telling Willie he'll get a medical discharge, but that doesn't seem to cheer him up. It's his father he's worried about, he told me. He also confessed that he thought we were going to beat him when he first came. I explained that we never beat anybody up because there's too much paperwork afterward if you leave marks. The other guys still call him a cocksucker, but I get the impression that he likes it here and wouldn't mind staying with us. "Even the cocksucker knows we got it made," Williams announces, and we all nod in agreement.

They took poor Willie away. That night it was snowing like hell, and the roads were in bad shape. Mace and I patrolled Luneville, but there were no GI's in town. We made the usual tour of the seedy bars, where all the whores were accounted for. It would have been a perfect night for listening to French torch songs on the old record player, but the jukeboxes were reserved for American pop and their French imitators. With no customers to worry about, the owners offered us drinks, and we accepted. Good cognac, not the rotgut they sell to the dumb soldiers. In one joint the madame even offered us girls, in the spirit of the holiday season, but we refused. Her whores looked like they must've been hustling when Gen. Patton passed through in 1944. They thought us refusing like that was very funny, and they made sucking noises with their lips, lifting their skirts to their crotches. They think the world of us since we broke up a bloody fight for them a couple of weeks ago. They know they can call us if some soldier gets nasty. We come and take him off by the scruff of his neck.

The snow was still coming down hard; even our jeep was slipping and sliding. We made one more stop, at the Café de la Gare. There was no one there except the boss and a couple of cab drivers waiting for the Paris train, which was late. Here, too, everyone was glad to see us. Drinks on the house—because of Mace, I thought to myself. The French have a thing about American blacks, especially when they're as tall and good-looking as Mace. Their own blacks they think are shit, but for Mace their eyes were full of admiration.

They wanted to know if we have such crummy weather where we come from. You bet, we told them. Ten times worse. That made them happy. Then the conversation turned to the subject of GI's, the way they behave in public places. They cause problems, we agreed; some of them are morons. They were glad to hear us say that. We made faces, and they made faces to emphasize the point. No doubt about it. The world is full of people like that.

In the seven months I've been in Toul and Luneville, I haven't met any girls. I talk to cops, whores, café owners, waiters, and the like, but that's as far as it goes. It is impossible to meet girls my age. Occasionally, I come across one and attempt to start a conversation. They reply briefly, politely, and suspiciously, and I get the impression they've been warned: if I catch you with an American, I'll kill you. Who can blame them?

Once in Nancy a family showed up at our downtown MP station—father, mother, and teenage daughter with a sizable belly—wanting to know about a certain corporal. We made a few calls and found out that the fellow had been discharged and was living somewhere in Oregon. All three of them hung their heads and stood there a long time, not knowing what to say or do next. They didn't have the vaguest idea where Oregon was. Finally, they shuffled out without another peep.

We have a new post commander. He barged into our quarters without a warning while we were still lazing in bed. It was almost noon. His eyes popped out when he saw the mess. Since my bunk is closest to the door, he started chewing me out first. Are you some kind of prima donna, he kept screeching over and over, as he poked with his foot at the dirty clothes on the floor. I never hung up any of my things, and nobody else did either. In my locker, where regulations specified my headgear should be, I kept bottles of wine. The other guys had beer. The upshot was, he would come back in three hours and the place would be so clean he could eat off the floor, or we would be in big trouble.

Well, we didn't bust our balls. We stuffed most of our things in the laundry bags and stashed them in our jeeps outside. When he returned, there were only a few items, properly displayed, to look at in our lockers. You could see he was puzzled but couldn't think of anything to say just then. Besides, there was the business of law and order to discuss. We exaggerated our problems—the continual knifings, so many fags running around, and so on. By now we were sitting in the station, beginning to relax a little around the elderly colonel. All of a sudden, he let out a shriek! We thought the Russians were at the door and looked in the direction he was pointing, but there was nothing to see. Just PFC Williams drinking water from a faucet.

"He is drinking French water!" the colonel screamed.

So what? We drink French water all the time, and it tastes really good. Would he like to try a glass?

He couldn't believe his ears! The whole United States Army could be incapacitated! What irresponsibility! The Commies would finally make that surprise attack starting World War III, and the American army would be in the latrine having the shits! He was going to put a stop to it right there and then.

He got on the phone, announced a national emergency, and ordered someone to bring us American water. They were to deliver a whole tanker of the best American water and leave it in the garage exclusively for our use. Anytime we were thirsty, we could just go out there and turn on the spigot. That way we would be safe, the army would be safe, and the Western democracies would be safe.

When he left we looked at each other in disbelief. You meet a lot of dummies among the officers, but this fellow topped them all. You watch, said Mace, this is not the end of it. There are plenty of other crazy notions where that one came from.

The tank of American water arrived. We all drank a glass just to see if there were any difference. There was none that we could tell. It was probably French water someone was passing off as American. There had to be a scam—but better that than the thought that they had ships crossing the Atlantic full of Jersey water.

The Poles came to ask us our opinion of the new colonel. He's a raving lunatic, we told them. They were delighted. It seems he had complained to their commander that the guards' shoes were not spit shined. These were fifty-year-old overweight alcoholics whom Stalin had sent to Siberia in 1939 and whom Gen. Andrews had rescued and led, via Persia and Egypt, into the battle for Italy in 1944; now an American colonel wanted them to spend their evenings spitting on shoes and polishing belt buckles!

And besides, outside it was sleeting and muddy.

I purchased an anthology of poetry, *Le Livre d'Or de la Poesie Française,* in a Luneville bookstore. The old sourpuss who owns the joint was surprised to see an MP buying a book like that. She gave me a searching look while handing me my change, suspicious and mystified. That pleased me immensely. I gave my best imitation of nonchalance as I walked slowly out and climbed into the jeep.

Cendrars was my man then. Described in the anthology as the "grand voyager," Cendrars abandoned his studies at the age of sixteen "pour courir le monde." I love his "Easter in New York" and his "Trans-Siberian Prose," which were included:

> En ce temps-là j'étais en mon adolescence.
> J'avais à peine seize ans et je me souvenais déjà plus de mon
>   enfance.
> J'étais à seize mille lieues du lieu de ma naissance.

If you don't watch it, Simic, I told myself, you're going to regress from being a super-modernist to a full-blooded Romantic!

True. A certain kind of sentimentality got to me. I had a great weakness, for instance, for the French popular singers of before the war: Frehel, Piaf, Lucienne Delyle, Lucienne Boyer. They made me wallow in self-pity, made me want to go AWOL and spend the rest of my life hiding in some Marseille dive, with a cigarette in the corner of my mouth, listening to a blind guy play the accordion. I could think of a dozen possible lives, each more heartbreaking than the other. While I listened to these songs, I wanted to be the bartender of that dive, in love with a streetwalker who was a cocaine addict but had a heart of gold.

In the meantime, my buddies told me I had a terrific future in police work. The New York Police Department would welcome me with open arms, thanks to my training and extensive experience. I would live like a king, taking bribes left and right, then retire to Florida after twenty years. They didn't realize I saw myself as a fall guy in one of these French songs I was listening to. I would spend the rest of my life in some seedy hotel off Place Blanche, reaching under the bed for a bottle of cheap red.

The French cops called us to say that a soldier had climbed the train station's roof and was trying to adjust the big hand of the clock. We went to see. They had to bring a fire truck with ladders to haul him down. He was still very drunk, but we asked him anyway why he had done it. The clock was five minutes fast, he told us.

Another call from the French, this time from the gendarmes who are the federal police: a longtime American deserter from a unit in Germany was apparently holed up in a hotel room in Épinal. We checked our files, found his name, and discovered that he was also believed to be extremely dangerous. That's what we told the gendarmes when we went to see them. They seemed delighted by the news. "Boom, boom," they shouted, winking and grinning at us. The plan was to arrive at the hotel at the crack of dawn when the deserter was in a deep sleep and break into his room with guns drawn.

We got to Épinal late, had a long supper with the gendarmes, and then went to their local station to wait for the morning. A long night of Sgt. Briggs's army and police stories, to which the French reciprocated with their own, all of which I had to translate.

There were two of us and four of them. It was past four o'clock. The French were loading their guns. That made me wide awake. I could imagine a gunfight and a stray bullet hitting me. The thought of firing myself worried me too. What if I killed someone? Every other time I had pulled the pistol in the past, it was to fire into the air. Then I had that option; this was different.

At the hotel the owner and his wife were waiting for us. They'd been warned. The deserter was asleep in his room on the second floor. We took off our boots, cocked our guns, and went up, one creaky stair after the other, the terrified owner right after us. On the second floor we came to a stop. Absolute silence. Winter. Snow outside.

We moved again, taking a long time to reach the door of room 17. One of the gendarmes was going to kick it in, and we were all going to rush in with guns pointed. The bed, we were told, was in the middle of the room facing the door.

Jesus! The noise as they broke in, with me lagging behind! In an instant the man in the bed had five guns pressed against his head. I thought his eyes would jump out of their sockets. We were all frozen like that for a minute or two, and then Briggs grabbed him by the hair, dragged him out of bed, threw him against the wall, kicked his legs apart, and started to search him. This seemed pointless to me; the poor guy had only a T-shirt and underwear on. No place to hide a weapon. Plus, he looked harmless. A tall, skinny fellow who may have been dying of starvation. The French, however, loved Briggs's rough stuff. "Comme chez nous," they squealed happily while nudging each other.

Well, it turned out the guy didn't even own a nail file. Nothing dangerous about him. He was a cook in some outfit in Germany. A religious nut. On the way to Nancy he told us about talking to God only last night. Briggs thought it was all an act. I didn't know what to think. He couldn't have been that innocent if he got as far as Épinal.

"Fuck them all!" Briggs says, and we all nod in agreement. We have no way to figure out why people act the way they do; we are not psychiatrists or father confessors. Our idea of happiness is: NOTHING HAPPENS. What others consider total boredom, we consider bliss. We get it, too. Three days go by without a single call. Everybody is behaving because the weather stinks. Let it stay like this forever. I've got my books; I've got my radio and my wine.

In two weeks I'm returning to my unit in Toul. I'll never be able to readjust to my regular army routine. Just to make my life miserable, the bastards there will make me direct traffic at the main gate the first day I get back. I'll wear white gloves and be expected to salute every officer in his car and be in every respect a model of military bearing and neatness.

I remember once being so hungover I didn't see the general—actually, I did see him but too late—and didn't salute. He got out of his car and dressed me down, while the traffic stood still and everyone sat in their vehicles enjoying themselves. The sergeant on duty screamed at me for half an hour when he found out what happened. The company commander yelled at me in front of the whole company the next day.

"Fuck them all," says Briggs again, and we all concur.

Briggs is going to marry his waitress, a big, strong widow with a couple of small kids. Not bad-looking, but, all the same, what is she going to do on a farm in South Dakota? They don't have a language in common. Briggs still hasn't learned more than two words of French, and her English is not much better.

On the other hand, the village she lives in is a dump. Only Mace loves the countryside around here: he wants to stay in Europe after he is discharged, travel, work, come back to France, eventually buy a small café with his savings.

"I'll spend the rest of my life visiting you guys," I tell them. I'll go see Williams and his whorehouse in LA, check out Briggs on his farm, visit Edwards in his shithole in South Carolina, and Mace himself will serve me Pernod when I drop by his café in St. Clement. They all love the idea, and we spend the rest of the evening imagining these visits, knowing all along that we'll never see each other again after we part company here.

Edwards never goes anywhere on his own. He doesn't understand why we do. "What's in Paris?" he wants to know. We tell him about the beauty of the city, the good-looking streetwalkers in furs, the nightclubs with nude dancing. "Nothing!" A waste of money, as far as he is concerned.

He's never been anywhere in the States either. We want to take him to a high-class restaurant in Luneville for a farewell dinner, but he's suspicious of French cooking. "It's better than the shit you eat at home," Mace tells him. He doesn't believe that for a moment. The Frenchies he sees on the base are not much to look at, poor farm folk from surrounding villages. Dressed half in their rags, half in our army clothes, they look like bums. When they grin, they usually have a couple of teeth missing. As for their patois, even I don't have a clue. Of course, they take home everything they can slip past the Poles at the gate, but who cares? From time to time we do a surprise stop and search, make them strip, collect piles of army clothes, equipment, tools, wire spoons, forks, everything but a tank! They stand there trembling in the cold, thinking they will lose their jobs, swearing by everything that's holy that they have no idea how the stuff got in their pockets. We tell them to forget it! No sweat. Uncle Sam is generous. Nothing to worry about. They can't believe their ears. Mouths hanging open in disbelief. Then an eruption! Joy! They want to hug and kiss us, take us home for a meal.

Anyway, these are the only French Edwards knows, and it takes us all day to convince him that he must come along and eat with us in Luneville. "It's an order," Briggs barks out finally, because Edwards keeps whining and changing his mind.

"Doesn't want to be seen with a nigger in a public place," is Mace's opinion. Could be.

Whatever the case, we drag the Carolina hick to the best restaurant in town, where we proceed to order a large, elegant meal. With Edwards, of course, we are extremely cautious: just steak and fries for the redneck. First, however, he has to try some smoked salmon. Again, a direct military order from his superior.

Edwards takes a teeny morsel, chews on it forever, then finally allows himself a little smile. He likes it! An order of your best smoked salmon just for Private Edwards, we yell to the waitress. Later he even confesses that he likes the fries. The best fries he ever had in his life! And the steak is good, too.

Now comes the hardest part. We have to make him take a sip of red wine. He won't hear of it. It's against his religious beliefs. "He thinks they were drinking Pepsi at the Last Supper," Mace says.

I have an idea, however. I notice Edwards is eyeing the pretty waitress, who keeps looking at him, too. I'm going to ask her to ask him to try the wine. That's what I do, in French so he doesn't understand. She goes over to him, pours the wine in his glass, and with the sexiest smile tells him that this wine is "very special" and would he please try it as a favor to her. Edwards sits there blushing, thinking it over. Then, all of a sudden, he picks up the glass, with all of us breathlessly watching, and takes a cautious sip. It's a miracle! We all applaud. "It's good," he says and takes a bigger sip. We are so happy we are kissing each other drunkenly. It's because we are not too far from Jeanne d'Arc's birthplace, I explain. The region is predisposed toward miracles, as you can see.

22

Sadness and good food are incompatible. The old sages knew that wine lets the tongue loose, but one can grow melancholy with even the best bottle, especially as one grows older. The appearance of food, however, brings instant happiness. A paella, a *choucroute garnie,* a pot of *tripes à la mode de Caen,* and so many other dishes of peasant origin guarantee merriment. The best talk is around the table. Poetry and wisdom are its company. The true muses are cooks. Cats and dogs don't stray far from the busy kitchen. Heaven is a pot of chili simmering on the stove. If I were to write about the happiest days of my life, many of them would have to do with food and wine and a table full of friends.

> Homer never wrote on an empty stomach.
>
> —Rabelais

One could compose an autobiography mentioning every memorable meal in one's life, and it would probably make better reading than what one ordinarily gets. Honestly, what would you rather have, the description of a first kiss or a stuffed cabbage done to perfection?

I have to admit, I remember better what I've eaten than what I've thought. My memory is especially vivid about those far-off days from 1944 to 1949 in Yugoslavia, when we were mostly starving. The black market flourished. Women exchanged their wedding rings and silk underwear for hams. Occasionally, someone invited us to an illicit feast on a day everyone else was hungry.

I'll begin with the day I realized that there was more to food than just stuffing yourself. I was nine years old. I ate Dobrosav

Cvetkovic's *burek*, and I can still see it and taste it when I close my eyes.

A *burek* is a kind of pie made with phyllo dough and stuffed with either ground meat, cheese, or spinach. It is eaten everywhere in the Near East and the Balkans. Like pizza today, it's usually good no matter where you get it, but it can also be a work of art. My father said that, when Dobrosav retired from his bakery in Skopje, the mayor and his cronies, after realizing that he was gone, sent a police warrant after him. The cops brought him back in handcuffs! "Dobrosav," they said, visiting him in jail, "how can you do a thing like that to us? At least make us one last *burek*, and then you can go wherever your heart desires."

I ate that famous *burek* forty-four years ago on a cold winter morning with snow falling. Dobrosav made it illegally in his kitchen and sold it to select customers, who used to knock on his door and enter looking like foreign agents making a pickup. The day I was his guest—for the sake of my poor exiled father, who was so good to Dobrosav—the *burek* came with meat. I ate every greasy crumb that fell out of my mouth on the table, while Dobrosav studied me the way a cat studies a bird in a cage. He wanted my opinion. I understood this was no fluke. Dobrosav knew something other *burek* makers did not. I believe I told him so. This was my first passionate outburst to a cook.

Then there was my aunt, Ivanka Bajalovic. Every time I wiped my plate clean she shook her head sadly. "One day," she'd say to me, "I'll make so much food you won't be able to finish it." With my appetite in those days, that seemed impossible, but she did it! She found a huge pot ordinarily used to make soap and filled it with enough beans to "feed an army," as the neighbors said.

All Serbs, of whatever gender or age, have their own opinion as to how this dish ought to be made. Some folks like it thick, others soupy. Between the two extremes there are many nuances. Almost everybody adds bacon, pork ribs, sausage, paprika, and hot peppers. It's a class thing. The upper classes make it lean, the lower fatty. My aunt, who was educated in London and speaks English with a British accent to this day, made it like a ditchdigger's wife. The beans were spicy hot.

My uncle was one of those wonders of nature everybody envies, a skinny guy who could eat all day long and never gain any weight. I'm sad to admit that I've no idea how much we actually ate that day. Anywhere between three and five platefuls is a good guess. These were European soup plates, nice and roomy, that could take loads of beans. It was a summer afternoon. We were eating on a big terrace watched by nosy neighbors, who kept score. At some point, I remember, I just slid off my chair onto the floor.

I'm dying, it occurred to me. My uncle was still wielding his spoon with his face deep in his plate. There was a kind of hush. In the beginning everybody talked and kidded around, but now my aunt was exhausted and had gone to lie down. There were still plenty of beans, but I was through. I couldn't move. Finally, even my uncle staggered off to bed, and I was left alone, sitting under the table, the heat intolerable, the sun setting, my mind blurry, thinking, this is how a pig must feel.

On May 9, 1950, I asked all my relatives to give me money instead of presents for my birthday. When they did, I spent the entire day going with a friend from one pastry shop to another. We ate huge quantities of cream puffs, custard rolls, *dobos torta,* rum balls, *pishingers,* strudel with poppy seed, and other Viennese and Hungarian pastries. At dusk we had no money left. We were dragging ourselves in the general vicinity of the Belgrade railroad station when a man, out of breath and carrying a large suitcase, overtook us. He wondered if we could carry it to the station for him, and we said we could. The suitcase was very heavy, and it made a noise as if it were full of silverware or burglar's tools, but we managed somehow to get it to his train. There he surprised us by paying us handsomely for our good deed. Without a moment's thought we returned to our favorite pastry shop, which was closing at that hour and where the help eyed us with alarm as we ordered more ice cream and cake.

In 1951 I lived an entire summer in a village on the Adriatic coast. Actually, the house my mother, brother, and I roomed at was a considerable distance from the village on a stretch of sandy beach. Our landlady, a war widow, was a fabulous cook. In her home I ate squid for the first time and began my lifelong love affair with olives. All her fish was grilled with a little olive oil, garlic, and parsley. I still prefer it that way.

My favorite dish was a plate of tiny surf fish called *girice*, which were fried in corn flour. We'd eat them with our fingers, head and all. Since it's no good to swim after lunch, all the guests would take a long siesta. I remember our deliciously cool room, the clean sheets, the soothing sound of the sea, the aftertaste and smell of the fish, and the long naps full of erotic dreams.

There were two females who obsessed me in that place. One was a theater actress from Zagreb in the room next to ours who used to sunbathe with her bikini top removed when our beach was deserted. I would hide in the bushes. The other was our landlady's sixteen-year-old daughter. I sort of tagged along with her. She must have been bored out of her wits to let a thirteen-year-old boy keep her company. We used to swim out to a rock in the bay where there were wild grapes. We'd lie sunbathing and popping the little blue grapes in our mouths. And in the evening, once or twice, there was even a kiss and then an exquisite risotto with mussels.

> He that with his soup will drink,
> When he's dead won't sleep a wink.
>
> —old French song

In Paris I went to what can only be described as a school for losers. These were youngsters who were not destined for the further glories in French education but were en route to being petty bureaucrats and tradespeople. We ate lunch in school, and the food was mostly tolerable. We even drank red wine. The vegetable soup served on Tuesdays, however, was out of this world. One of the fat ladies I saw milling in the kitchen must have been a southerner, because the soup had a touch of Provence. For some reason the other kids didn't care for it. Since the school rule was that you had to manger everything on your plate, and since I loved the soup so much, my neighbors at the table would let me have theirs. I'd end up eating three or four servings of that thick concoction with tomatoes, green and yellow beans, potatoes, carrots, white beans, noodles, and herbs.

After that kind of eating, I usually fell asleep in class after lunch, only to be rudely awakened by one of my teachers and ordered to a blackboard already covered with numbers. I'd stand there bewildered and feeling sleepy, while time changed into eternity and nobody budged or said anything. My only solace was the lingering taste in my mouth of that divine soup.

Some years back I found myself in Genoa at an elegant reception in Palazzo Doria talking with the Communist mayor. "I love American food," he blurted out to me after I mentioned enjoying the local cuisine. I asked him what he had in mind. "I love potato chips," he told me. I had to agree, potato chips were pretty good.

When we came to the United States in 1954, it now seems as if that's all my brother and I ate. We sat in front of the TV eating potato chips out of huge bags. Our parents approved. We were learning English and being American. It's a wonder we have any teeth left today. We visited the neighborhood supermarket twice a day to sightsee the junk food. There were so many things to taste, and we were interested in all of them. There was deviled ham, marshmallows, Spam, Hawaiian Punch, Fig Newtons, V-8 Juice, Mounds Bars, Planter's Peanuts, and so much else, all good. Everything was good in America except Wonder Bread, which we found disgusting.

It took me a few years to come to my senses. One day I met Angelo. He told me that I ate like a dumb shit and took me home to his mother. Angelo and his three brothers were all well employed, unmarried, living at home, and giving their paychecks to Mom. The father was dead, so there were just these four boys to feed. She did not stop cooking. Every meal was like a peasant wedding feast. Of course, her sons didn't appreciate it, as far as she was concerned. "Are you crazy, Mom?" they'd shout in a chorus each time she brought in another steaming dish. The old lady didn't flinch. The day I came she was happy to have someone else at the table who was more appreciative, and I did not spare the compliments.

She cooked southern Italian dishes. Lots of olive oil and garlic. I recollect with a sense of heightened consciousness her linguine with anchovies. We drank red Sicilian wine with it.

She'd put several open bottles on the table before the start of the meal. I never saw anything like it. She'd lie to us and say there was nothing more to eat, so we'd have to eat at least two helpings, and then she'd bring out some sausage and peppers and after that some kind of roast.

After the meal we'd remain at the table, drinking and listening to old records of Beniamino Gigli and Feruccio Tagliavini. The old lady would still be around, urging on us a little more cheese, a little more cake. And then, just when we thought she had given up and gone to bed, she'd surprise us by bringing out a dish of fresh figs.

My late father, who never in his life refused another helping at the table, had a peculiarity common among gastronomes. The more he ate the more he talked about food. My mother was always amazed. We'd be done with a huge turkey roasted over sauerkraut, and my father would begin reminiscing about a little breakfastlike sausage he'd had in some village on the Romanian border in 1929 or a fish soup a blind woman made for him in Marseilles in 1945. Well, she wasn't completely blind, and besides she was pretty to look at—in any case, after three or four stories like that we'd be hungry again. My father had a theory that, if you were still hungry, say for a hot dog, after a meal at Lutèce, that meant that you were extraordinarily healthy. If a casual visitor to your house was not eating and drinking three minutes after his arrival, you had no manners. Of people who had no interest in food, he had absolutely no comprehension. He'd ask them questions like an anthropologist, and go away seriously puzzled and worried. He told me toward the end of his life that the greatest mistake he ever made was accepting his doctor's advice to eat and drink less after he passed seventy-five. He felt terrible until he went back to his old ways.

One day we were walking up Second Avenue and talking. We get into this elaborate philosophical argument, as we often do. I feel as if I've understood everything! I'm inspired! I'm quoting Kant, Descartes, Wittgenstein, when I notice he's no longer with me. I look around and locate him a block back staring into a shop window. I'm kind of pissed, especially since I have to walk back to where he's standing, since he doesn't move or answer my shouts. Finally, I tap him on the shoulder, and he looks at me, dazed. "Can you believe that?" he says and points to a window full of Hungarian smoked sausages, salamis, and pork rinds.

My friend Mike DePorte, whose grandfather was a famous St. Petersburg lawyer and who in his arguments combines a Dostoyevskian probity with his grandfather's jurisprudence, claims that such an obsession with food is the best proof we have of the existence of the soul. Ergo, long after the body is satisfied, the soul is not. "Does that mean," I asked him, "that the soul is never satisfied?" He has not given me his answer yet. My own notion is that, when the souls are happy, they talk about food.

23

Thirty years ago in New York City I used to stay up late almost every night listening to Jean Shepherd's rambling soliloquies on the radio. He had a show with a lot of interesting talk and a little music. One night he told a lengthy story, which I still remember, about the sacred ritual of some Amazon tribe. It went roughly like this.

Once every seven years the members of this remote tribe would dig a deep hole in the jungle and lower their finest flute player into it. He would be given no food, only a little water and no way of climbing out. After this was done, the other members of the tribe would bid him good-bye, never to return. Seven days later the flute player, sitting cross-legged at the bottom of his hole, would begin to play. Of course, the tribesman could not hear him, only the gods could, and that was the point.

According to Shepherd, who was not above putting on his audience of insomniacs, an anthropologist had hidden himself during the ritual and recorded the man playing the flute. Tonight Shepherd was going to play that very tape.

I was spooked. Here was a man, soon to die, already dizzy with hunger and despair, summoning whatever strength and belief in gods he had. A New World Orpheus, it occurred to me.

Shepherd went on talking until finally, in the wee-hour silence of the night and my shabby room on East Thirteenth Street, the faint sound of the otherworldly flute was heard: its solitary, infinitely sad squeak with the raspy breath of the living human being still audible in it from time to time, making the best of his predicament. I didn't care then, nor do I care now whether Shepherd made up the whole story. We are all at the bottom of our own private pits, even here in New York.

All the arts are about our impossible predicament. That's their fatal attraction. "Words fail me," poets often say. Every poem is an act of desperation or, if you prefer, a throw of the dice. God is the ideal audience, especially if you can't sleep or if you're in a hole in the Amazon. If he's absent, so much the worse.

The poet sits before a blank piece of paper with a need to say many things in the small space of the poem. The world is huge, the poet is alone, and the poem is just a bit of language, a few scratchings of a pen surrounded by the silence of the night.

It could be that the poet wishes to tell you about his or her life. A few images of some fleeting moment when one was happy or exceptionally lucid. The secret wish of poetry is to stop time. The poet wants to retrieve a face, a mood, a cloud in the sky, a tree in the wind, and take a kind of mental photograph of that moment in which you as a reader recognize yourself. Poems are other people's snapshots in which we recognize ourselves.

Next, the poet is driven by the desire to tell the truth. "How is truth to be said?" asks Gwendolyn Brooks. Truth matters. Getting it right matters. The realists advise: open your eyes and look. People of imagination warn: close your eyes to see better. There's truth with eyes open, and there's truth with eyes closed, and they often do not recognize each other on the street.

Next, one wishes to say something about the times in which one lives. Every age has its injustices and immense sufferings, and ours is scarcely an exception. There's the history of human vileness to contend with, and there are fresh instances every day to think about. One can think about it all one wants, but making sense of it is another matter. We live in a time in which there are hundreds of ways of explaining the world. Everything from every variety of religion to every species of scientism is believed. The task of poetry, perhaps, is to salvage a trace of the authentic from the wreckage of religious, philosophical, and political systems.

Next, one wants to write a poem so well crafted that it would do honor to the tradition of Emily Dickinson, Ezra Pound, and Wallace Stevens, to name only a few masters.

At the same time, one hopes to rewrite that tradition, subvert it, turn it upside down, and make some living space for oneself.

At the same time, one wants to entertain the reader with

outrageous metaphors, flights of imagination, and heartbreaking pronouncements.

At the same time, one has, for the most part, no idea of what one is doing. Words make love on the page like flies in the summer heat, and the poem is as much the result of chance as it is of intention. Probably more so.

This is a small order from a large menu requiring one of those many-armed Indian divinities to serve as a waiter.

One great defect of poetry, or one of its sublime attractions— depending on your view—is that it wants to include everything. In the cold light of reason, poetry is impossible to write.

The predictions of poetry's demise, about which we so often read, are plain wrong, just as most of the intellectual prophecies in our century have been wrong. Poetry proves again and again that any single overall theory of anything doesn't work. Poetry is always the cat concert under the window of the room in which the official version of reality is being written. The academic critics write, for instance, that poetry is the instrument of the ideology of the ruling class and that everything is political. The tormentors of Anna Akhmatova are their patron saints. But what if poets are not crazy? What if they convey the feel of a historical period better than anybody else? Obviously, poetry engages something essential and overlooked in human beings, and it is this ineffable quality that has always ensured its longevity. "To glimpse the essential . . . stay flat on your back all day, and moan," says E. M. Cioran. There's more than that to poetry, of course, but that's a beginning.

Lyric poets perpetuate the oldest values on earth. They assert the individual's experience against that of the tribe. Emerson claimed that to be a genius meant "to believe your own thoughts, to believe that what is true for you in your private heart is true for all men." Lyric poetry since the Greeks has always assumed something like that, but American poetry since Whitman and Emerson has made it its main conviction. Everything in the world, profane or sacred, needs to be reexamined repeatedly in the light of one's own experience.

Here, now, I am amazed to find myself living my life . . . The American poet is a modern citizen of a democracy who lacks any clear historical, religious, or philosophical foundation. Sneering Marxists used to characterize such statements as "typical bourgeois individualism." "They adore the smell of their own shit," a fellow I used to know said about poets. He was a Maoist, and the idea of each human being finding his or her own truth was incomprehensible to him. Still, this is what Robert Frost, Charles Olson, and even Elizabeth Bishop had in mind. They were realists who had not yet decided what reality is. Their poetry defends the sanctity of that pursuit in which reality and identity are forever being rediscovered.

It's not imagination or identity that our poets primarily trust, but examples, narratives, or specific experiences. There's more than a little of the Puritan diarist still left in poets. Like their ancestors, they worry about the state of their inner lives in between entries about the weather. The problem of identity is ever present, as is the nagging suspicion that one's existence lacks meaning. The working premise, nevertheless, is that each self, even in its most private concerns, is representative, that the "aesthetic problem," as John Ashbery has said, is a "microcosm of all human problems," that the poem is a place where the "I" of the poet, by the kind of visionary alchemy, becomes a mirror for all of us.

"America is not finished, perhaps never will be," Whitman said. Our poetry is the dramatic knowledge of that state. Its heresy is that it takes a part of the truth for the whole truth and makes it a "temporary stay against confusion," in Robert Frost's famous formulation. In physics it is the infinitely small that contradicts the general law, and the same is true of poetry at its best. What we love in it is its democracy of values, its recklessness, its individualism, and its freedom. There's nothing more American and more hopeful than its poetry.

The black dog on the chain wags his tail as I walk by. The house and the barn of his master are sagging, as if about to collapse with the weight of the sky. On my neighbor's porch and in his yard there are old cars, stoves, refrigerators, washing machines, and dryers that he keeps carting back from the town dump for some unclear and still undecided future use. All of it is broken, rusty, partly dismantled, and scattered about, except for the new-looking and incongruous plaster statue of the Virgin with eyes lowered, as if embarrassed to be there. Past his house there's a spectacular winter sunset over the lake, the kind one used to see in paintings sold in the back of discount department stores. As for the flute player, I remember reading that in the distant Southwest there are ancient matchstick figures on the walls of desert caves and that some of them are playing the flute. In New Hampshire, where I am now, there's only this dark house, the ghostly statue, the silence of the woods, and the cold winter night falling down in a big hurry.

24

Late one night, as the half-moon rode high above the Church of St. Mark, I grabbed my balls while passing a priest. This happened in Belgrade when I was twelve years old. I was skipping along without a care in the world when he came around the corner. He assumed I was about to greet him—he was even inclining his head benevolently—then I did what my friends advised me to do when meeting a priest. He stood there steaming in his cassock for a moment. Then it was my turn to be surprised. Plump as he was, he went after me with extraordinary quickness, waving his arms about and shouting: "You little creep! You little son of a bitch!" His cussing terrified me even more than the chase he gave me. I ran without looking back.

At home the photographs of my great-great-grandfathers and uncles awaited me on the living room walls. On my mother's side I had several priests and one bishop in my ancestry. I've never seen a wanted poster with a more murderous collection of mugs. They had huge black-and-white beards that grew even sideways. Their eyes were bulging. The photographer must have warned them not to move, and they obeyed. Flies crawled inside of their ears during the long exposure. Their noses itched terribly. That evening, after seeing the priest, their eyes followed me with unusual grimness. They all knew what I had done.

The meanest looking of the lot was my grandfather's father. It was public knowledge that his children hated him. My grandfather did not permit any mention of priests or religion in our house when he was around. When my grandmother died, he informed the family that there would be no priest officiating in the cemetery or at the grave site. A scandal, people whispered. Everybody crossed themselves just thinking about it. A couple of aunts decided to disobey his wishes. The priest would appear at the grave site while the coffin was being lowered, and my grandfather, so the theory went, would be too overwhelmed with grief and sorrow to object to a short prayer being said.

That's not what happened. Just as the grave diggers were fussing with the ropes and the family and friends were standing with bowed heads, the priest materialized in his vestments, a prayer book in hand, already blessing us and mumbling a prayer. To everyone's astonishment, Grandpa lunged at him. Before we had time to realize what was happening, the old curmudgeon had the priest by the scruff of the neck and was marching him away from the grave. As if that weren't enough, one of my weeping aunts ran after them, grabbed the tails of grandfather's coat, and started pulling him back. She had the strength of ten, and so did he. A tug of war ensued and lots of yelling. The old man was trying to kick her without turning and letting the priest go. Unfortunately, my mother rushed my brother and me away before we could see and hear more.

If you had asked anybody in my family if God exists, they would have given you a puzzled look. Of course he does, they would have replied. This meant, in practice, attending the church only to baptize, wed, and bury someone. Bona fide atheists probably mention religion and God more frequently than my mother ever did. My father, however, was a different story. He didn't mind entering churches. Russian churches, black churches, old Italian churches, austere New England churches, Byzantine churches—all were admirable. The same is true of me. He liked the pomp and music, but he liked an empty church even more. A few times I saw him get down on his knees to pray, but he had no use for organized religion or for any other idea that sought to take its place. As far as he was concerned, communism and fascism were versions of the nastiest aspects of Christianity. "All that orthodoxy, fanaticism, virtue by decree," he'd complain. They were all enemies of the individual, forever peddling intolerance and conformity. He had serious philosophical interest in Islam, Buddhism, Hinduism, and Christianity but no desire to join any congregation of the faithful. Belief in God was something private, like sex. If you did not believe in anything, as I often told him was the case with me, that was all right, too.

"Come on," she yanked my arm. "Let's go. They're just a couple of hicks," she assured me, but I had to take a better look at the street preachers.

The young woman with thick glasses pressed a Bible to her heart; the horse-faced fellow by her side strummed a tuneless guitar at the edge of a large Saturday night crowd. They preached and sang hymns as if dogs were biting their asses.

My friend had had enough. Without my noticing, she split. I was left in the custody of their Jesus, who, by the sound of it, had too many lost sheep already to worry about. His great love always spurned—"Sweet Jesus," they hollered, trying to drown out an ambulance crying its heart out somewhere in the dark city beyond the brightly lit movie houses and penny arcades all around us.

Hell! I was deeply moved.

America is God crazy, as everyone knows. It's impossible to be an American writer without taking that into account.

Driving just after daybreak early one spring morning through West Virginia, I'm listening to the radio. Someone is playing scratchy old black gospel records. The station is fading and coming clear in turn; the car is speeding down the empty road, and I'm wondering who is choosing records so impeccably, so mysteriously, given the odd hour. Beyond the enjoyment, the emotion is gripping me, and I have a sudden realization: they mean every word they say. Every word. They sing so beautifully, and so wildly, because they believe the Lord is in their midst right then and there.

It has always seemed obvious to me that we are alone in the universe. I love metaphysics and its speculations, but the suspicion at the core of my being is that we are whistling in the dark. Still, I have tears in my eyes every time I hear good church music. Never has the human heart been so pure, I think. Perhaps divinity can only be experienced by those who sing together? The God who comes or who does not come to the solitaries is a different one.

"Without the mystery, the most incomprehensible of all, we are incomprehensible to ourselves," said Pascal, in a different context.

Sing and shout, Reverend! is my advice. Do that little dance step, while the choir behind you sways and slaps its tambourines and the old lady on the piano and the scrawny kid on the electric guitar nod to each other with approval. There's no doubt about it: "Except for music, everything is a lie," as Cioran says.

One day I finally admitted to myself that I'm hopelessly superstitious. You do not believe in God, I said to myself, so how come you believe in bad luck? I have no reply to that. Do we make our Fate, or is our Fate an independent agency? Calvin at least knew who arranged our destiny; I do not.

This head of mine is full of contradictions, teetering on two legs; is this the modern version of holy foolishness? Let's hope so.

In the meantime, the worries of a crumb overlooked on death's dinner plate . . .

I was always attracted to mystical and esoteric doctrines that propose the unknowingness of the Supreme Being, the ineffability of the experience of his presence, and the ambiguity of our human condition. Ambiguity, that great carnivore. If I believe in anything, it is the dark night of the soul. Awe is my religion, and mystery is its church. I include here equally the mysteries of consciousness and the torments of the conscience.

If not for conscience, would we ever consider the possibility of the independent existence of evil? Nothing explains the world and the people in it. This is the knowledge that makes us fall down on our knees and listen to the silence of the night. Not even a dog or an owl is brave enough to interrupt it tonight. Being and nothingness, those two abstractions, how real, how close, they feel. In such moments I want to reach for my chessboard. Let them play each other, and I'll sit and watch until the first streak of light slips under the door and crawls to my feet without waking the dust.

Many years ago Vasko Popa took me to visit the women's monastery Mesić, near his hometown, Vršac, on the Yugoslav-Romanian border. We had a long lunch at a young poet's house and did not leave till five in the afternoon. I don't remember much about the drive, since we were talking a lot, interrupting each other with stories and jokes; but all of a sudden there was a high wall at the end of a dirt road and a closed iron gate. We left the car outside the gate and pushed it open just enough to squeeze through. What we found inside was a veritable jungle, as if the grass had not been cut all summer and the trees had grown wild over the years without being trimmed and thinned out. We followed what was once a road and now a narrow path in the twilight calm broken occasionally by the sound of a bird or cricket. We did not speak. After a mile or so, we saw through the trees several large houses and a small Byzantine church. We walked to the largest of them, knocked, opened the door, peeked inside, and even announced ourselves; but only silence came out to welcome us. It was so quiet, our steps became cautious. We walked on tiptoe on the way to the next house. Through the open door we could see six nuns sitting in a circle with heads bowed. Vasko knew the name of the prioress and called out to her. She jumped, and the nuns followed after her in joy and delight to see him. The prioress, who was old, used to be in her youth a lady-in-waiting at the royal court, Vasko had told me, and was exceptionally well educated. Vasko sent her French books. She was just reading Camus and immediately wanted to talk about him with us.

We were given a tour by the prioress and a tall, skinny young nun. We visited the church, which was under repair, to see some surprisingly fine frescoes, and then slowly, because of the prioress's age we climbed to the small graveyard above the church. The sun had just set. "I'll be soon resting here," the prioress told us, laughing. We smiled in reply. One could almost envy the prospect.

Then we were led back to the large house we had first come to. This we heard was one of the local bishop's many summer residences. He had not stayed in it for the last thirty years, but everything was kept in readiness for his arrival. We sat in a large living room with the prioress and the skinny nun drinking home-made brandy while being sternly examined by the former bishops in sooty old paintings. Only one table lamp had been lit. Vasko talked, and so did the old woman, but the rustling of so many leaves muffled their voices, and then all of a sudden there was complete silence. Here was peace of a world outside time, the kind one encounters in fairy-tale illustrations, in which a solitary child is seen entering a dark forest of gigantic trees.

After a while I listened only to the silence deepen; the night continued to hold its breath.

"Every poem, knowingly, or unknowingly, is addressed to God," the poet Frank Samperi told me long ago. I remember being surprised, objecting, mentioning some awful contemporary poems. We were filling subscription cards in the stockroom of a photography magazine and having long philosophical conversations on the subject of poetry. Frank had been reading a lot of Dante, so I figured, that's it. He is stuck in fourteenth-century Italy.

No more. Today I think as he did then. It makes absolutely no difference whether gods and devils exist or not. The secret ambition of every true poem is to ask about them even as it acknowledges their absence.

25

... the tongue we use
When we don't want nuance
To get in the way.

—Cornelius Eady

At the end of a murderous century, let's curse the enemies of the individual.

Every modern ideologue and thought policeman continues to say that the private is political, that there is no such thing as an autonomous self, and, if there is, for the sake of the common good it is not desirable to have one. He or she who refuses to accept the idea that the self is socially constructed and that it can be manipulated to fit the latest theory of human improvement is everywhere the enemy. In the academy of lies where new enthusiasms and hatreds are being concocted, where "only children and madmen speak the truth," as Goebbels said, the unrepentant individual is the one standing in the corner with his or her face to the wall. Orthodoxy, groupthink, virtue by decree, are ideals of every religion and every utopian model of society. The only intellectual problem that the philosophers of such systems have is how to make conformism attractive. Ideologies from nationalism to racism are not really about ideas; they're revivalists' tents offering the righteous a chance to enjoy their sense of superiority. "We will find eternal happiness and harmony by sacrificing the individual," every congregation of the faithful continues to rhapsodize.

Historical experience has taught me to be wary of any manifestation of collectivism. Even literary historians and critics, when they generalize, make me suspicious. Of course, young poets and painters do associate and influence each other and partake of the same zeitgeist, but, despite these obvious truths, what literature worth anything is written by a group? Has any genuine artist ever thought of himself or herself exclusively as a part of a movement? Is anyone seriously a postmodernist, whatever that is?

I don't find systems congenial. My aesthetic says that the poet is true because he or she cannot be labeled. It is the irreducible uniqueness of each life that is worth honoring and defending. If at times one has to fall back on the vocabulary of abuse to keep those in the gumming business away, so be it.

The first and never-to-be-forgotten pleasure that language gave me was the discovery of "bad words." I must've been three or four years old when I overheard my mother and another woman use the word *cunt*. When I repeated it to myself, when I said it aloud for all to hear and admire, I was slapped by my mother and told never to use that word again. Aha, I thought, there are words so delicious they must not be said aloud! I had a great-aunt who used to use such language every time she opened her mouth. My mother would beg her, when she came to visit, not to speak like that in front of the children, but she paid her no mind. To have a temper and a foul mouth like that was a serious liability in a Communist country. "We'll all end up in jail because of her," my mother said.

There are moments in life when true invective is called for, when there comes an absolute necessity, out of a deep sense of justice, to denounce, mock, vituperate, lash out, rail at, in the strongest possible language. "I do not wish to be weaned from this error," Robert Burton wrote long ago in his *Anatomy of Melancholy*. I agree. If anything I want to enlarge and perfect my stock of maledictions.

This is what I learned from twentieth-century history: only dumb ideas get recycled. The dream of a social reformer is to be the brains of an enlightened, soul-reforming penitentiary. Everyone vain, dull, peevish, and sexually frustrated dreams of legislating his impotence. Mao's uniforms: a billion dressing the same and shouting from his little red book continues to be the secret hope of new visionaries.

Once one comes to understand that much of what one sees and hears serves to make fraud sound respectable, one is in trouble. For instance, long before Parisian intellectuals did so, my great-aunt, Nana, had figured out that the Soviet Union and the so-called people's democracies were a scam and a lie from the bottom up. She was one of these women who see through appearances instantly. To begin with, she did not have a good opinion of humanity. Not because she was a sourpuss, a viper's nest of imaginary resentments. Far from it. She liked eating, drinking, a good laugh, and a quick roll in the hay behind her elderly husband's back. It's just that she had an unusually uncluttered and clear head. She would tell you that our revolutionary regime, which regarded loose tongues and levity as political crimes and those unfortunates caught in the act as unhealthy elements, was a huge pile of shit, and that included Marshal Tito himself. Her outbursts were caused by what she regarded as other people's gullibility. As far as she was concerned, cowards and dunces surrounded her. The daily papers and the radio drove her into verbal fury. "Admit it," she'd yell at my mother and grandmother. "Doesn't it turn your stomach to hear them talk like that?"

If they agreed and confided in a whisper that, yes, indeed, these Commies are nothing but a bunch of murderous illiterate yokels, Stalinists stooges, and whatnot, she still wasn't happy. There was something about humans as a species that worried her no end. It's not like they were different yesterday and the day before yesterday. This frenzy of vileness and stupidity started on day one. She'd throw her hands up in the air in despair again and again. She couldn't get over it. It was like she had an incurable allergy to everything false and slimy. It didn't lessen her zest for life, because she had a way of exorcizing these evil spirits, but it was a full-time job. Cursing them, I imagine, gave her royal pleasure and, unknown to her, me too, listening behind the closed door with a shameless grin.

In a book entitled *Paradoxes of Gender* Judith Lorber gives us a feminist version of this recurring madness:

> In a world of scrupulous gender equality, equal numbers of girls and boys would be educated and trained for the liberal arts and for the sciences, for clerical and manual labor and for all profes-

sions. Among those with equal credentials, women and men would be hired in an alternating fashion for the same types of jobs—or only men hired to do women's types of jobs until half of every workplace was made of men and half, women. ([New Haven: Yale University Press, 1994], 58)

Very nice, one thinks, but what about the cops, the jailers, and the informers needed to enforce all of this? Will they be organized in units composed with strict gender equality? We hope so. Note, as is typical of all-pious hypocrites and prophets of universal happiness, there's no mention of the individual.

How are we to defend ourselves against these monsters dividing the members of society into useful and useless? For them the ideal citizen is a voluntary slave! America, or any other place on earth, must be a school of virtue where even the political meaning of a sunset in a poem will be carefully examined for unauthorized views!

I knew a thirteen-year-old who wrote a letter telling off President Johnson about the conduct of the Vietnam War. It was some letter: our president was an idiot and a murderer who deserved to be napalmed himself, and worse. One evening as the boy and his mother and sister, who told me the story, were sitting around the kitchen table slurping their soup, the doors and the windows leading to the fire escape opened at the same time and men with drawn guns surrounded the table. "We are the FBI," they announced, and they wanted to know, who was Anthony Palermo? The two women pointed at the boy with thick glasses and crossed eyes. Well, it took a while to convince them that he was the one who wrote the letter. They were expecting a full-grown Commie assassin with long hair and an arsenal of weapons and bombs by his side.

"What do you want from me, blood?" I heard an old woman shout once in a welfare office. She kept cussing them for another five minutes, not because she had any expectations that the wrongs done to her would be righted but simply in order to make herself feel good and clean for one brief moment.

26

It is the night again around me; I feel as though there had
been lightning—for a brief span of time I was entirely in my
element and in my light.

—Nietzsche

The mind loves the unknown. It loves images whose
meaning is unknown, since the meaning of the mind itself is
unknown.

—Magritte

I wore Buster Keaton's expression of exaggerated calm. I
could've been sitting on the edge of a cliff with my back to the
abyss trying to look normal.

Now I read philosophy in the morning. When I was younger
and lived in the city, it was always at night. "That's how you
ruined your eyes," my mother kept saying. I sat and read late
into the night. The quieter it got, the more clearheaded I
became—or so it seemed to me. In a sparsely furnished room
above an Italian grocery, I would be struggling with some intri-
cate philosophical argument that promised a magnificent in-
sight at its conclusion. I could sense it with my whole being. I
couldn't put the book away, and it was getting really late. I had
to be at work in the morning. Even had I tried to sleep, my head
would've been full of Kant or Hegel. So, I wouldn't sleep. At
some point I'd make that decision. I'd be sitting there with the
open book, my face reflected dimly in the dark windowpane, the
great city all around me grown quiet. I was watching myself
watch myself. A very strange experience.

The first time it happened I was twenty. It was six o'clock in
the morning. It was winter. It was dark and very cold. I was in
Chicago riding the El to work seated between two heavily

bundled-up old women. The train was overheated, but, each time the door opened at one of the elevated platforms, a blast of cold air would send shivers through us. The lights, too, kept flickering. As the train changed tracks, the lights would go out for a moment, and I would stop reading the history of philosophy I had borrowed from the library the previous day. "Why is there something rather than nothing?" the book asked, quoting Parmenides. It was as if my eyes were opened. I could not stop looking at my fellow passengers. How incredible, I thought, all of us being here, existing.

Philosophy is like a homecoming. I have a recurring dream about the street where I was born. It is always night. I'm walking past vaguely familiar buildings trying to find our house, but somehow it is not there. I retrace my steps on that block of only a few buildings, all of which are there except the one I want. The effort leaves me exhausted and saddened.

In another version of the same dream, I catch a glimpse of our house. There it is, at last, but for some reason I'm unable to get any closer to it. No lights are on. I look for our window, but it is even darker there on the third floor. The entire building seems abandoned. "It can't be," I tell myself in horror.

Once in one of these dreams, many years ago, I saw someone at our window, hunched over as if watching the street intently. That's how my grandmother would wait late into the night for us to come home, except that this was a stranger. Even without being able to make out his face, I was sure of that.

Most of the time, however, there's no one in sight during the dream. The facades of buildings still retain their pockmarks and other signs of the war. The streetlights arc out, and there's no moon in the sky, so it's not clear to me how I am able to see all this in complete darkness. The street I am walking on is long, empty, and seemingly without end.

Whoever reads philosophy reads himself as much as he reads the philosopher. I am in dialogue with certain decisive events in my life as much as I am with the ideas on the page. Meaning is the matter of my existence. My effort to understand is a perpetual circling around a few obsessive images.

Like everyone else, I have my hunches. All my experiences make a kind of untaught ontology, which precedes all my readings. What I am trying to conceptualize with the help of the philosopher is that which I have already intuited.

That's one way of looking at it.

> The Meditation of yesterday filled my mind with so many doubts that it is no longer in my power to forget them. And yet, I do not see in what manner I can resolve them; and, just as if I had all of a sudden fallen into very deep water, I am so disconcerted that I can neither make certain of setting my feet on the bottom, nor can I swim and so support myself on the surface. I shall nevertheless make an effort and follow anew the same path as that on which I yesterday entered, i.e., I shall proceed by setting aside all that in which the least doubt could be supposed to exist, just as if I had discovered that it was absolutely false; and I shall ever follow in this road until I have met with something which is certain, or at least, if I can do nothing that is certain. Archimedes, in order that he might draw the terrestrial globe out of its place, and transport it elsewhere, demanded only that one point should be fixed and immovable; in the same way I shall have the right to conceive high hopes if I am happy enough to discover one thing only which is certain and indubitable.

I love this passage of Descartes—his beginning again, his not wanting to be fooled. It describes the ambition of philosophy in all its nobility and desperation. I prefer this doubting Descartes to the later one, famous in his certainties. The poetry of indeterminacy still casts its spell. Of course, he's greedy for the absolute, but so is everyone else. Or are they?

There's an Eastern European folk song that tells of a girl who kept tossing an apple higher and higher until she tossed it as high as the clouds. To her surprise the apple didn't come down. One of the clouds got it. She waited with arms outstretched, but the apple stayed up there. All she could do was plead with the clouds to return her apple, but that's another story. I like the first part when the impossible still reigns.

I remember lying in a ditch and staring at some pebbles while German bombers were flying over our heads. That was long ago.

I don't remember the face of my mother nor the faces of the people who were there with us, but I still see those perfectly ordinary pebbles.

"It's not 'how' things are in the world that is mystical, but that it exists," says Wittgenstein. I felt precisely that. Time had stopped. I was watching myself watching the pebbles and trembling with fear. Then time moved on, and the experience was over.

The pebbles stayed in their otherness, stayed forever in my memory. Can language do justice to such moments of heightened consciousness? Speech is always less. When it comes to conveying what it means to be truly conscious, one approximates, one fails miserably.

Wittgenstein puts it this way: "What finds its reflection in language, language cannot represent. What expresses 'itself' in language, we cannot express by means of language." This has been my experience many times. Words are impoverishments, splendid poverties.

I knew someone who once tried to persuade me otherwise. He considered himself a logical positivist. These are people who remind you, for example, that you can speak of a pencil's dimension, location, appearance, and state of motion or rest but not of its intelligence and love of music. The moment I hear that, the poet in me rebels and I want to write a poem about an intelligent pencil in love with music. In other words, what these people regard as nonsense, I suspect to be full of imaginative possibilities.

There's a wonderful story told about Wittgenstein and his Cambridge colleague, the Italian economist Piero Sraffa. Apparently, they often discussed philosophy. "One day," as Justus Hartnack has it, "when Wittgenstein was defending his view that a proposition has the same logical form as the fact it depicts, Sraffa made a gesture used by Neopolitans to express contempt and asked Wittgenstein's own recollection, it was this question which made him realize that his belief that a fact could have a logical form was untenable."

As for my "logical" friend, we argued all night. "What cannot be said, cannot be thought," he claimed. And then—after I blurted out something about silence being the language of consciousness—"You're silent because you have nothing to say!" In any case, it got to the point where we were calling each other "you dumb shit." We were drinking large quantities of red wine, misunderstanding each other totally, and only stopped bickering when his disheveled wife came to the bedroom door and told us to shut up.

Then I told him a story.

One day in Yugoslavia, just after the war, we made a class trip to the town War Museum. At the entrance we found a battered old German tank, which delighted us. Inside the museum one could look at a few rifles. Hand grenades and uniforms but not much else. Most of the space was taken up by photographs. These we were urged to examine. One saw people who had been hanged and people about to be hanged. The executioners stood around smoking. There were piles of corpses everywhere. Some were naked. Men and women with their genitals showing. That made some kids laugh.

Then we saw a man having his throat cut. The killer sat on the man's chest with a knife in his hand. He seemed pleased to be photographed. The victim's eyes I don't remember. A few men stood around gawking. There were clouds in the sky.

There were always clouds, blades of grass, tree stumps, bushes, and rocks no one was paying any attention to. In one photograph the earth was covered with snow. A miserable, teeth-chattering January morning and someone making someone else's life even more miserable. Or the rain would be falling. A small, hard rain that would wash the blood off the hands immediately, that would make one of the killers catch a bad cold. I imagined him sitting that same night with feet in a bucket of hot water and sipping tea.

That occurred to me later. Now that we had seen all there was to see, we were made to sit on the lawn outside the museum and eat our lunch. It was poor fare. Most of us had plum jam spread on slices of bread. A few had lard sprinkled with paprika. One kid had nothing but bread and scallions. I guess that's all they had at his home that day. Everybody thought it was funny. Someone snatched his thick slice of black bread and threw it up in the air. It got caught in a tree. The poor kid tried to get it down by throwing stones at it. He kept missing. Then he tried climbing the tree. He kept sliding back. Even our teacher, who came to see what the commotion was all about, thought it was hilarious.

As for the grass, there was plenty of it, each blade distinct and carefully sharpened, as it were. There were also clouds in the sky and many large flies of the kind one encounters in slaughter-houses, which kept pestering us and interrupting our laughter.

And here's what went through my head just last night as I lay awake thinking of my friend's argument:

The story you told him had nothing to do with what you were talking about.

The story had everything to do with what we were talking about.

I can think of a hundred objections after all these years.

Only idiots want something neat, something categorical—and I never talk unless I know!

Aha! You're mixing poetry and philosophy. Wittgenstein wouldn't give you the time of day!

"Everyone looks very busy to me," says Jasper Johns, and that's my problem, too.

I remember a strange cat, exceedingly emaciated, that scratched on my door the day I was scratching my head over Hegel's Phenomenology of the Spirit.

Who said, "Whatever can be thought must be fictitious"?

You got me there! How about a bagel Hegel?

Still and all . . . And above all! Let's not forget "above all."

Here's what Nietzsche said to the ceiling: "The rank of the philosopher is determined by the rank of his laughter." But he couldn't really laugh.

I know because I'm a connoisseur of paradox. All the good-looking oxymorons are in love with me and come to visit me in my bed at night.

Try a tomato Plato!

Wallace Stevens has several beautiful poems about solitary readers. "The House Was Quiet and the World Was Calm" is one. It speaks of a "truth in a calm world." It happens! The world and the mind growing so calm that truth becomes visible.

It must be late at night "where shines the light that lets be the things that are"—the light of insomnia. The solitude of the reader of philosophy and the solitude of the philosopher drawing together. The impression that one is thinking and anticipating another man's subtlest turns of thought and beginning to truly understand.

Understanding depends on the relationship of what we are to what we have been: the being of the moment. Consciousness stirring up our conscience, our history. Consciousness as the light of clarity and history as the dark night of the soul.

The pleasures of philosophy are the pleasures of reduction—the epiphanies of hinting in a few words at complex matters. Both poetry and philosophy, for instance, are concerned with Being. What is a lyric poem, one might say, but the re-creation of the experience of Being. In both cases, that need to get it down to its essentials, to say the unsayable and let the truth of Being shine through.

History, on the other hand, is antireductive. Nothing tidy about it. Chaos! Bedlam! Hopeless tangle! My own history and the history of this century like a child and his blind mother on the street. She mumbles, talks to herself, sings, and wails as she leads the way across some busy intersection.

You'd think the sole meaning of history is to stand truth happily upon its head!

Poor poetry. Like imperturbable Buster Keaton alone with the woman he loves on an ocean liner set adrift on the stormy sea. Or an even better example: again drifting over an endless ocean, he comes across a billboard, actually a target for battleship practice. Keaton climbs it, takes out his fishing rod and bait, and fishes peacefully. That's what great poetry is. A superb serenity in the face of chaos. Wise enough to play the fool.

And always the contradictions: I have Don Quixote and his windmills in my head and Sancho Panza and his mule kicking in my heart.

That's just some figure of speech. Who could live without them? Do they tell the truth? Do they conceal it? I really don't know. That's why I keep going back to philosophy. I want to learn how to think clearly about these matters.

It is the morning. It is night. The book is open. The text is difficult; the text is momentarily opaque. My mind is wandering. My mind is struggling to grasp the always elusive, the always hinting—whatever it is.

It, it, I keep calling it. An affinity of "it" without a single antecedent—like a cosmic static in my ear.

Just then, about to give up, I find the following on a page of Heidegger: "No thinker has ever entered into another thinker's solitude. Yet it is only from its solitude that all thinking, in a hidden mode, speaks to the thinking that comes after or that went before."

For a moment it all comes together: poetry, philosophy, history. I see—in the sense of being able to picture and feel—the human weight of another's solitude. So many of them seated with a book. Day breaking. Thought becoming image. Image becoming thought.

27

The year is 1942 or 1943, and this is one of my earliest memories. I think it was winter. My mother had taken me to the opera, to a performance of Mozart's *Marriage of Figaro*. It's the first act, and Susanna and Figaro are in an eighteenth-century salon, pacing up and down. On several tables there are candelabra with lit candles. At one point Susanna brushes against one of the candles, and the long scarf she is wearing over her shoulders catches fire. The audience gasps. She stops singing and stands clutching her head in terror while the flames get bigger and bigger. Figaro, without missing a beat, quickly snatches the scarf, throws it on the floor, and stamps on it like a Spanish dancer. All along he's singing that beautiful music . . .

—1985–90